TOTALLY BEADS

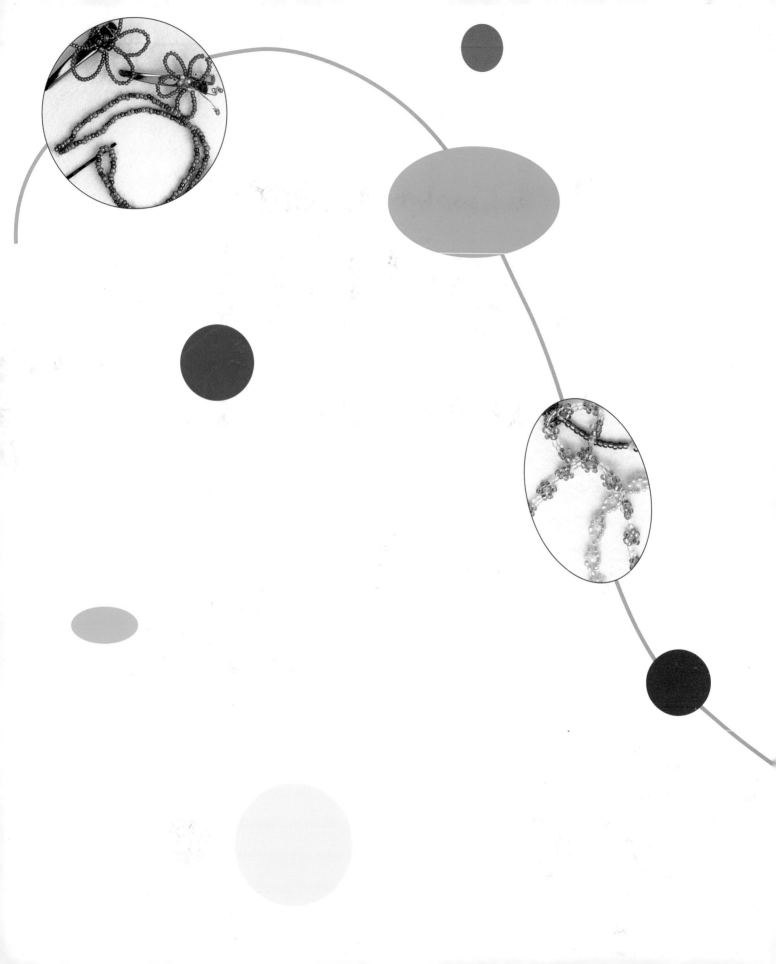

TOTALLY
BEADS

Sonal Bhatt

Sterling Publishing Co., Inc.
New York

To Mom, Dad, and Rupal,
with all my love and thanks.

Photography by Michael Hnatov Studios. Edited by Isabel Stein.
Book Design by Carol Malcolm Russo/Signet M Design, Inc.

Library of Congress Cataloging-in-Publication Data

Bhatt, Sonal
    Totally beads / by Sonal Bhatt.
      p. cm.
    ISBN 0-8069-7911-9
      1. Beadwork–Juvenile literature. [1. Beadwork. 2. Handicraft.] I. Title.

TT860 .B49 2001
745.58'2–dc21

                                         2001031316

1 3 5 7 9 10 8 6 4 2

Published by Sterling Publishing Company, Inc.
387 Park Avenue South, New York, N.Y. 10016
© 2001 by Sonal Bhatt
Distributed in Canada by Sterling Publishing
C/o Canadian Manda Group, One Atlantic Avenue, Suite 105
Toronto, Ontario, Canada M6K 3E7
Distributed in Great Britain and Europe by Chris Lloyd at Orca Book Services,
Stanley House, Fleets Lane, Poole BH15 3AJ, England
Distributed in Australia by Capricorn Link (Australia) Pty Ltd.
P.O. Box 704, Windsor, NSW 2756, Australia
Printed in China

Sterling ISBN 0-8069-7911-9

CONTENTS

THE BASICS
7

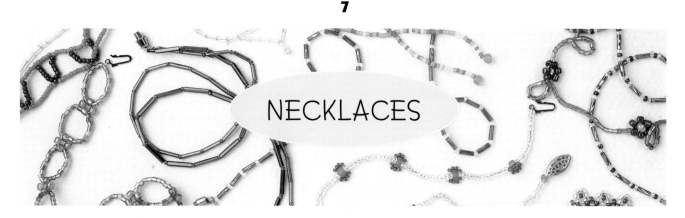

NECKLACES

Simply beads necklace, **14** • Twice as nice necklace, **15** • Floating beads necklace, **16** • Two-tailed necklace, **17** • Curling tail necklace, **18** • Circles necklace, **20** • Hanging bugle beads necklace, **22** • Sunshine necklace, **24** • Hanging loops necklace, **26** • Linking loops necklace, **28** • Icicles necklace, **30** • Multi-strand choker, **32** • Flowers and leaves necklace, **34** • Flowers out of line, **36**

BRACELETS AND ANKLETS

Zigzag flowers bracelet, **40** • Crossing strands bracelet, **42** • Coiled snake bracelet, **43** • Chain of flowers bracelet, **44** • Squares bracelet, **46** • Diamonds bracelet, **48** • Triangles bracelet, **50** • Techno triangles bracelet, **52** • Waves and pearls anklet, **54** • Hanging circles anklet, **56**

HAIR ORNAMENTS

Braided headband, **60** • Roman headband, **62** • Twister barrette, **63** • Bugle bead stripes barrette, **64** • Festive stripes barrette, **66** • Beaded bobby pin, **68** • Dangling bug bobby pin, **69** •. Dangling beads bobby pin, **70** • Squiggles bobby pin, **71** • Hanging wire star bobby pin, **72** • Wire flower bobby pin, **74** • Wire butterfly bobby pin, **76** • Dragonfly bobby pin, **78**

INDEX
80

THE BASICS

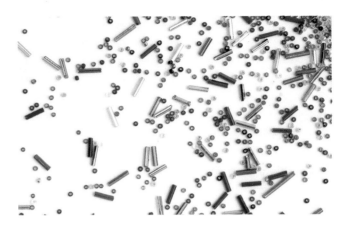

Welcome to the wonderful world of beading. The beauty of beading is that even with the simplest patterns, you can make amazing things. Beads are like words: put them together and you can make poetry. Start by visiting a bead store. Explore. Look at all the amazing colors, shapes, and sizes. Hold them in your hands to see how they feel. Imagine what you are going to say with beads. This book is a beginning. Once you learn how to make these patterns, experiment to create your own. Who knows what fantastic pieces you can create! Let's get started....

- Seed beads are small round glass or plastic beads used for many of the patterns in this book. They are size 11/0. Their diameter is about 1.5 mm or 16 to the inch.
- e beads are size 6° or 6/0 round glass or

BEADS

Beads come in a variety of colors, shapes, and sizes. The most common sizes that I used are size 11° (also written 11/0) and size 6° or 6/0. Beads are usually measured in millimeters (mm).

Some beads used in the projects. Left back: e beads. Left front: Seed beads. Right: Long and short bugle beads.

There are 25 mm to an inch. You can use a metric ruler to get an idea of the sizes if you are unfamiliar with them. Here are some beads we use in the projects:

plastic beads that are larger than seed beads, about 4 mm in diameter or about 6 to the inch. They are sometimes called small pony beads.

• Bugle beads are tubular plastic or glass beads that are measured by their length. We will use ⅛" (3 mm), ¹⁄₁₆" (1.5 mm), and ½" (13 mm) bugle beads.

There are many types of bead beyond these. Once you have learned how to do the patterns in this book, try replacing some beads with other types. Use your imagination and vary colors and patterns to match your mood or your clothes.

Supplies include thread, fine wire, beeswax, and glue.

THREADS

It's important to use thread that is both strong and thin. For many of the patterns, the thread will have to go through a bead more than once. Try to use a thread thickness of .5 mm or thinner. If you use bead thread without a needle for a project, it's a good idea to dab the ends in a little glue to make a stiff tip for the thread before starting. This will make the thread easier to string through the beads and will keep the thread ends from unraveling. Another good option is clear nylon monofilament thread, which is both strong and flexible. A third choice is very thin wire, such as 26-gauge wire. If you use wire, you don't need a needle. The higher the gauge, the thinner the wire. Most of the

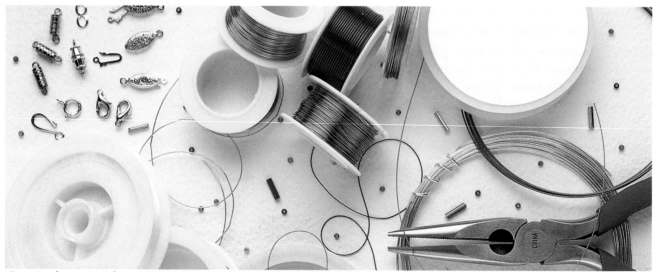

Catches (upper left) and various kinds of monofilament thread and wire, plus pliers for bending heavy wire.

projects in this book, except the ones with flowers (Flowers and Leaves, Flowers Out of Line, Zigzag Flowers, Chain of Flowers) can be made with either thread or 26-gauge wire. The Coiled Snake Bracelet uses 18-gauge wire, which is a bit thicker. Don't use wire for patterns that call for elastic, however.

Some the patterns in the book—for example, the headbands—call for a stretchy, elastic thread. This comes in many colors and thicknesses. For stringing seed beads, use a thread of thickness .5 mm or smaller. When using elastic thread, it may be useful to put a little beeswax on the thread to keep it from catching on itself.

NEEDLES

Needles are optional for many of the patterns in this book, but you may find that having a needle is helpful when you have to pass the thread through a bead more than once. Beading needles can be found in many craft stores. Most are flexible and have small eyeholes. There are also those with collapsible eyeholes, useful for thicker threads. These, however, are sometimes too flexible and therefore difficult to use.

CLASPS OR CATCHES

There are a variety of clasp types you can use. The symbol for clasp in this book is a yellow square. The symbol for a knot is a small black dot.

Barrel clasps, which look like little barrels and screw together, are good for necklaces and

A variety of clasps, used for necklaces and bracelets.

anklets, but not so good for bracelets, because they are hard to put on with one hand. For bracelets, use other types of clasp. Choose elastic thread if you don't want to use a clasp at all.

OTHER STUFF YOU WILL NEED

For some of these projects you will be using barrettes (hair clasps) and bobby pins (hairpins). For wire projects with thick wire, you will also need to use a pair of long-nose pliers to bend the wire, and something to cut the wire, like nail clippers or wire cutters.

Barrette with Twister bead design attached.

KNOTS

Anytime you start or finish a bead project using thread, you will have to make knots to secure the beads. Double overhand knots are the easiest to make. Practice these:

• An overhand knot is made like a loop with a thread through it (**Fig. 1**).

Fig. 1. Overhand knot.

• A double knot is made by passing the thread through a loop like an overhand knot, and repeating the step again (**Fig. 2**).

Fig. 2. Double knot.

• Use overhand knots to attach clasps to threads (**Fig. 3**).

Fig. 3. Attaching thread to a clasp with a double overhand knot.

• If you will be making a necklace with 2 strands, you can use a multiple-strand knot (**Fig. 4**).

Fig. 4. Knot to attach 2-stranded necklace to a clasp.

• Beware—knots can come undone! It is best to protect your knots by dabbing a little strong white glue or craft glue on them with a toothpick. Clear nail polish also works. Use a glue that is washable, clear, and suitable for use on the type of thread you chose. Check with the manufacturer if you are not sure.

THREAD OR WIRE ENDS

You can trim these fairly short, but the best thing to do is to leave a tail of 2" to 3" (5 to 7 cm) when starting out before tying on your thread. When you finish beading, put the thread tail through a second needle, run it back through a few beads at the end of the project, tie it a few times between two beads, and then clip off the excess thread tail. This will make your work stronger and neater. We will call this process "neatening ends" from now on to avoid having to describe it over and over. If you use wire, secure it by twisting a tail of about 1" (2.5 cm) around the main wire 4 or 5 turns with your fingers or a pliers, just before the start of the beading (**Fig. 5**) to neaten ends. Finish the project in the same way. Trim off the excess wire ends, and be sure a wire end is not sticking out so it doesn't poke anyone.

Fig. 5

WHAT IF YOU RUN OUT OF THREAD IN THE MIDDLE OF THE PROJECT?

- If it seems you will run out of thread in the middle of the project, stop beading about 4" (10 cm) from the end of the thread.
- Loop the thread back around and through the last bead you put on (**Fig. 6a**).
- Secure this thread with a double knot (**Fig. 6b**).
- Pull tight!
- Tie a double knot in a new piece of thread and string it through the last bead you added (**Fig. 6c**). Pull this thread tight against the bead, and continue beading. If possible, work the tail end back through the previous beads with a needle, and tie it between two beads to hide the end. Otherwise snip the tail end short.

Now that we know the basics, let's start beading!

Fig. 6a

Fig. 6b

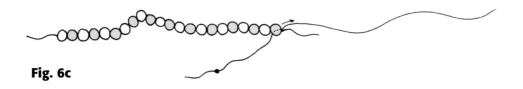

Fig. 6c

NECKLACES

Simply Beads Necklace

You Will Need

Clear seed beads
Black seed beads
Light purple bugle beads, ½″ (13 mm)
Thread
Clasp
Needle (optional)

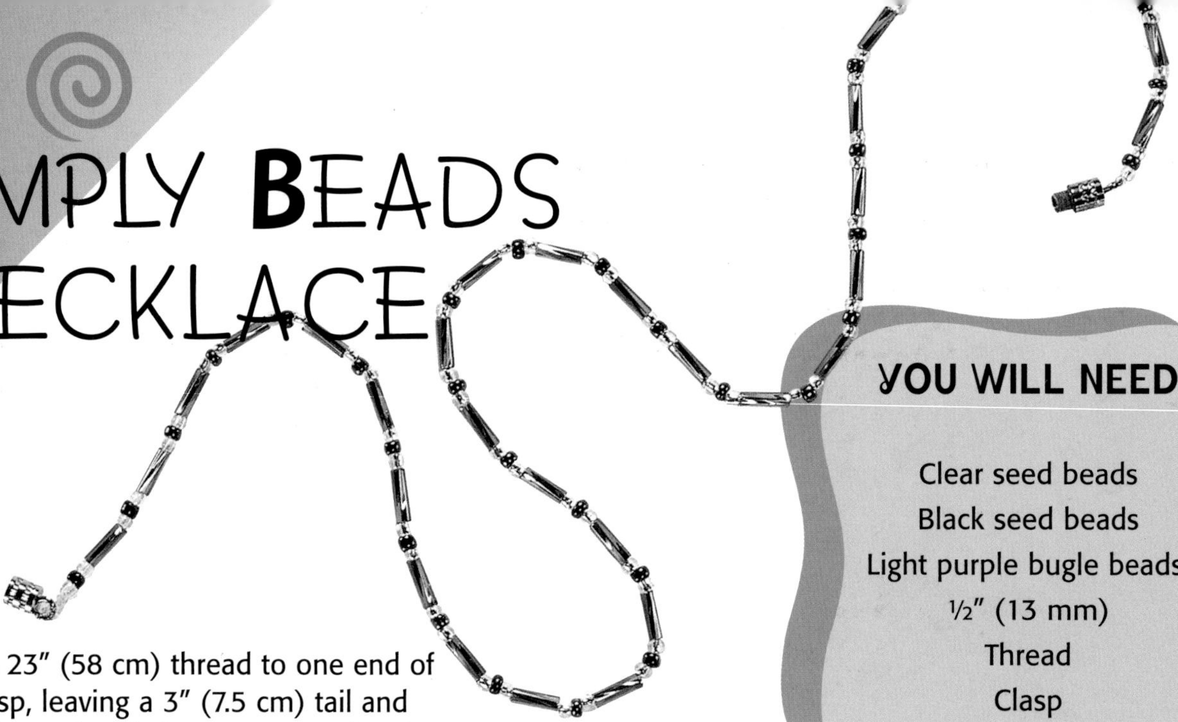

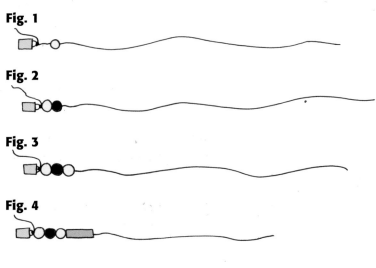

1. Tie a 23″ (58 cm) thread to one end of a clasp, leaving a 3″ (7.5 cm) tail and making a double knot (two overhand knots) with the short end of the thread.
2. String one clear seed bead (**Fig. 1**).
3. String one black seed bead (**Fig. 2**).
4. Add a clear seed bead (**Fig. 3**).
5. Next string a purple bugle bead (**Fig. 4**).
6. Again string one clear, one black, one clear seed bead, and then a purple bugle bead (**Fig. 5**).
7. Continue this pattern until you get a length that fits comfortably around your neck.
8. Finish by tying on the second end of the clasp with a double knot, and neaten the ends.

Fig. 1

Fig. 2

Fig. 3

Fig. 4

Fig. 5

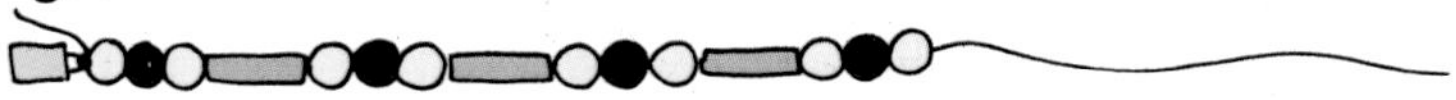

TWICE AS **N**ICE **N**ECKLACE

YOU WILL NEED

Green seed beads
Blue seed beads
Blue bugle beads,
½" (13 mm)
Green bugle beads,
½" (13 mm)
Thread
Clasp
Needle

1. Tie on a clasp end at the center of a 36" (91 cm) thread.

2. On the top thread, add a green seed bead and then a blue bugle bead. Continue this pattern until the strand fits around your neck (**Fig. 1**). Finish by tying on the other end of the clasp.

Fig. 1

3. On the second thread, add one blue seed bead and then one green bugle bead. Continue this pattern until this strand is 1" (2.5 cm) longer than the top strand (see **Fig. 2,** bottom). Finish by tying the second strand to the end of the clasp. Neaten ends.

Fig. 2

FLOATING BEADS NECKLACE

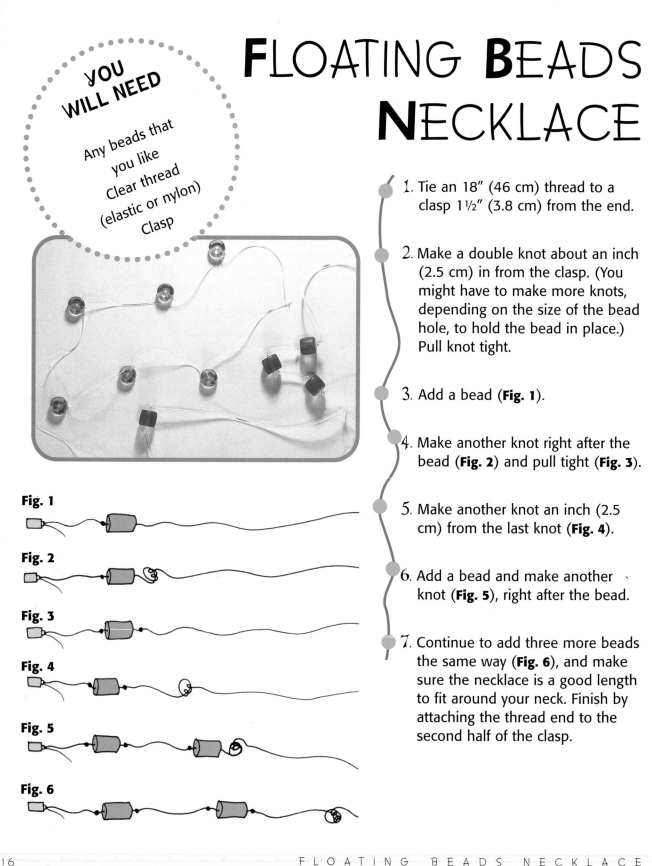

Fig. 1

Fig. 2

Fig. 3

Fig. 4

Fig. 5

Fig. 6

1. Tie an 18" (46 cm) thread to a clasp 1½" (3.8 cm) from the end.

2. Make a double knot about an inch (2.5 cm) in from the clasp. (You might have to make more knots, depending on the size of the bead hole, to hold the bead in place.) Pull knot tight.

3. Add a bead (**Fig. 1**).

4. Make another knot right after the bead (**Fig. 2**) and pull tight (**Fig. 3**).

5. Make another knot an inch (2.5 cm) from the last knot (**Fig. 4**).

6. Add a bead and make another knot (**Fig. 5**), right after the bead.

7. Continue to add three more beads the same way (**Fig. 6**), and make sure the necklace is a good length to fit around your neck. Finish by attaching the thread end to the second half of the clasp.

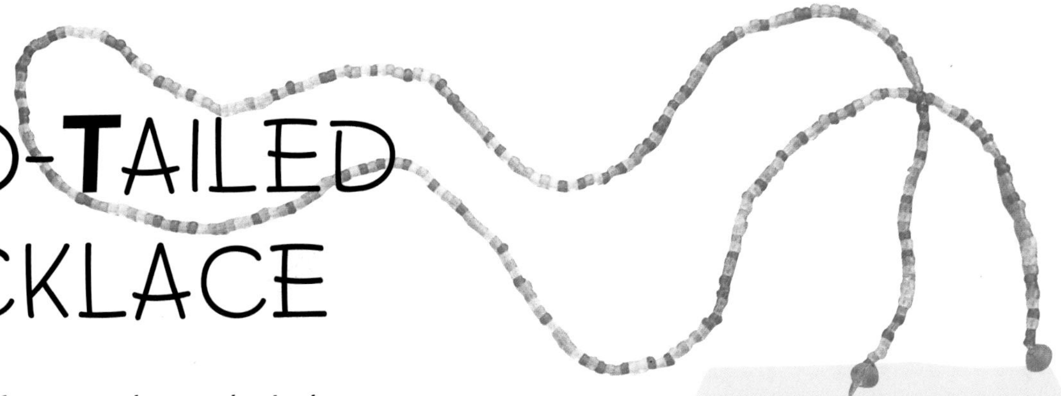

TWO-TAILED NECKLACE

1. Take beads of 3 or 4 colors and mix them together in a bowl. As you make this necklace, randomly select beads to put on the string.

2. Tie a temporary knot at one end and string just seed enough beads onto a 21" (53 cm) thread to fit around your neck (**Fig. 1**).

3. Once your strand is long enough, push the beads to center, leaving equal amounts of empty thread on each side. Trim off the temporary knot.

4. Put the threads together and string two more beads (**Fig. 2**).

5. Separate the strands and add more seed beads (**Fig. 3**) to each thread for a few inches (6 or 7 cm). Add an e bead to the end of each thread, and tie knots to secure the beads. Trim off excess thread.

YOU WILL NEED

3 or 4 colors of seed beads
Matching color of e beads
Elastic thread
Needle (optional)

TRY THIS
Make your necklace tails longer, vary the colors, or make a single tail.

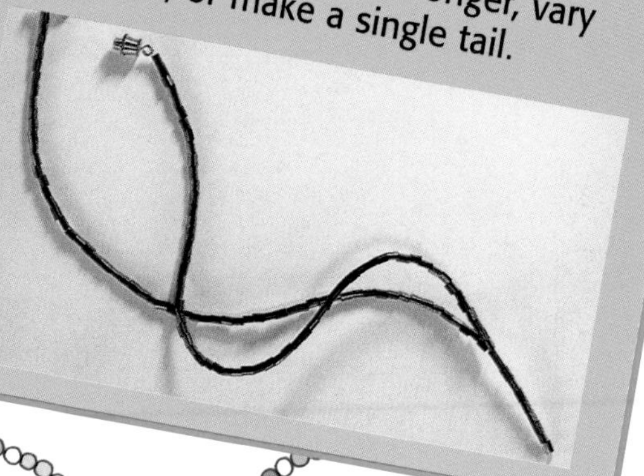

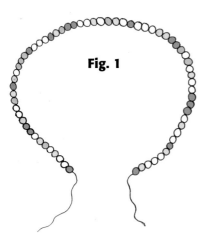

Fig. 1

Fig. 2

Fig. 3

Curling Tail Necklace

Fig. 1

1. Three inches (7.5 cm) from the end, attach a clasp end to a 23" (58 cm) thread.

2. String enough orange beads to make a strand that fits around your neck. Make sure the total number of beads is an odd number. Finish by tying the thread to the other end of the clasp (**Fig. 1**).

TRY THIS
Use small (¼" or 6 mm) bugle beads instead of seed beads to make the necklace.

Fig. 2

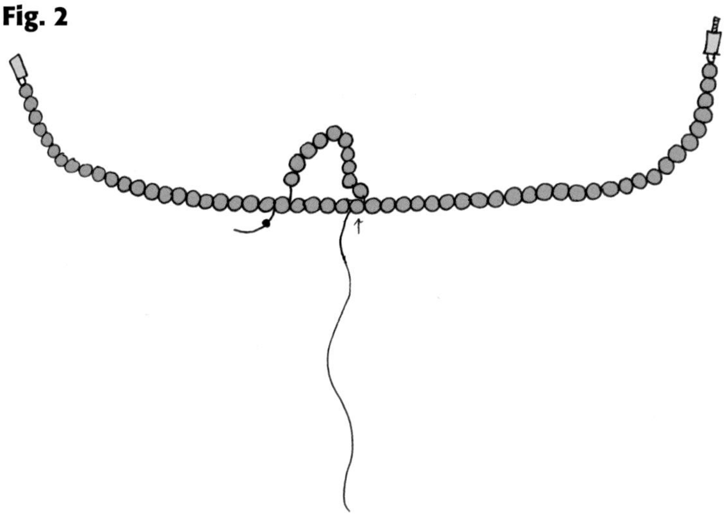

3. Count the beads and find the center bead. Mark it with a bit of tape or thread. String another thread 15″ (38 cm) long through the bead that is 5 beads to the left of the center bead, and then string on 10 to 15 orange seed beads and pass the thread down through the center bead (**Fig. 2**).

Fig. 3

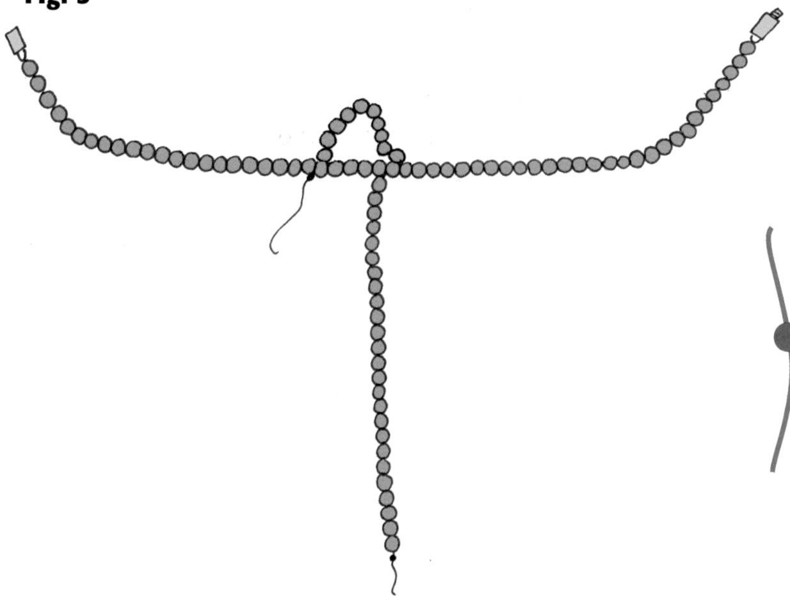

4. Add 25 beads, and then secure at the bottom with a double knot (**Fig. 3**). Neaten ends.

CIRCLES NECKLACE

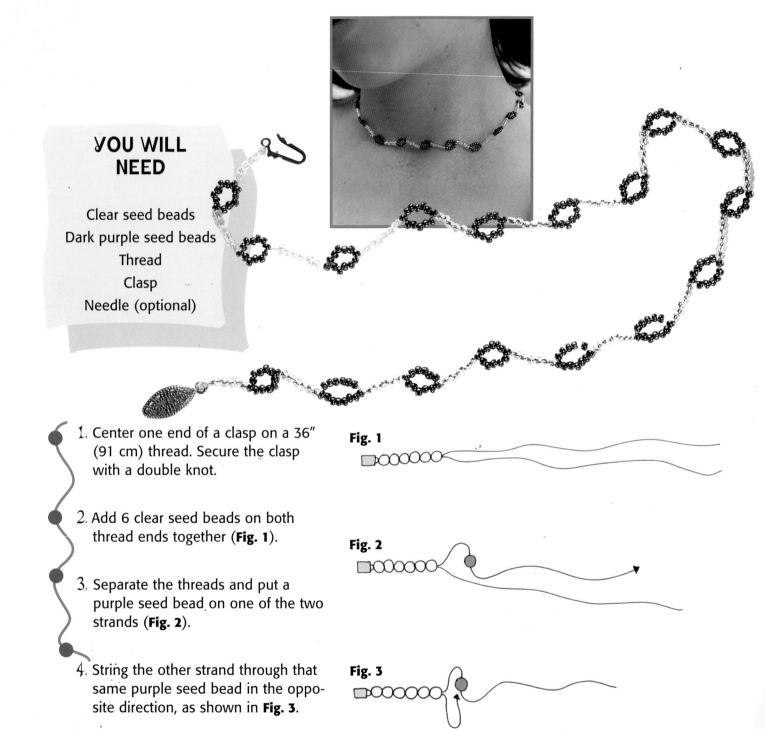

YOU WILL NEED

Clear seed beads
Dark purple seed beads
Thread
Clasp
Needle (optional)

1. Center one end of a clasp on a 36" (91 cm) thread. Secure the clasp with a double knot.

2. Add 6 clear seed beads on both thread ends together (**Fig. 1**).

3. Separate the threads and put a purple seed bead on one of the two strands (**Fig. 2**).

4. String the other strand through that same purple seed bead in the opposite direction, as shown in **Fig. 3**.

Fig. 1

Fig. 2

Fig. 3

5. Pull tight (**Fig. 4**).

Fig. 4

6. Add 5 purple seed beads to each thread (**Fig. 5**).

Fig. 5

7. Add another purple seed bead to one of the strands (**Fig. 6**).

Fig. 6

8. String the other thread through the same purple seed bead in the opposite direction (**Fig. 7**).

Fig. 7

9. Pull tight, and then add 6 more clear seed beads (**Fig. 8**).

Fig. 8

10. Continue the pattern until you get a length that fits around your neck. Finish by tying on the other end of the clasp. Neaten the ends.

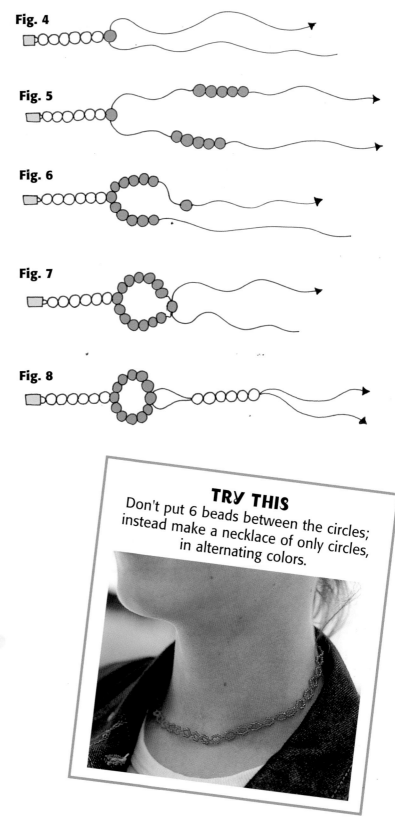

TRY THIS
Don't put 6 beads between the circles; instead make a necklace of only circles, in alternating colors.

HANGING BUGLE BEADS NECKLACE

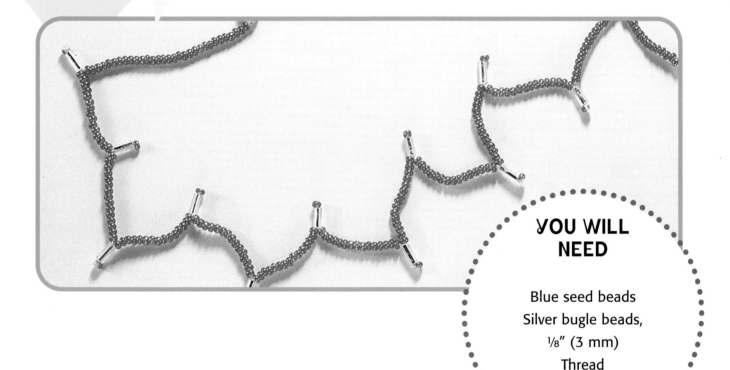

1. Tie a clasp to a 21" (53 cm) thread 2½" (6 cm) from the end.

2. String 15 blue seed beads (**Fig. 1**).

Fig. 1

3. Add one silver bugle bead (**Fig. 2**).

Fig. 2

4. Add another blue seed bead (**Fig. 3**) and push all the beads together so there are no spaces between beads.

Fig. 3

5. String the thread back through the bugle bead in the opposite direction (**Fig. 4**).

Fig. 4

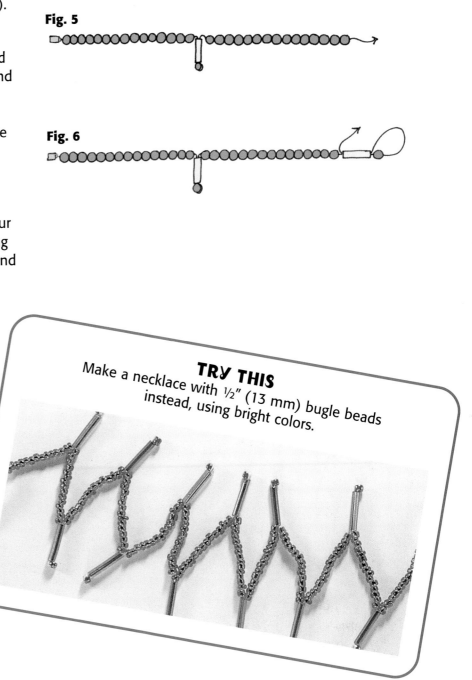

6. Add 15 blue seed beads (**Fig. 5**).

Fig. 5

7. String one silver bugle bead and add another blue seed bead, and push all beads together. String the thread back through the bugle bead, only in the opposite direction (**Fig. 6**).

Fig. 6

8. Continue the pattern until you get a length that fits around your neck comfortably. Finish by tying on the other end of the clasp and neatening the ends.

TRY THIS

Make a necklace with ½" (13 mm) bugle beads instead, using bright colors.

SUNSHINE NECKLACE

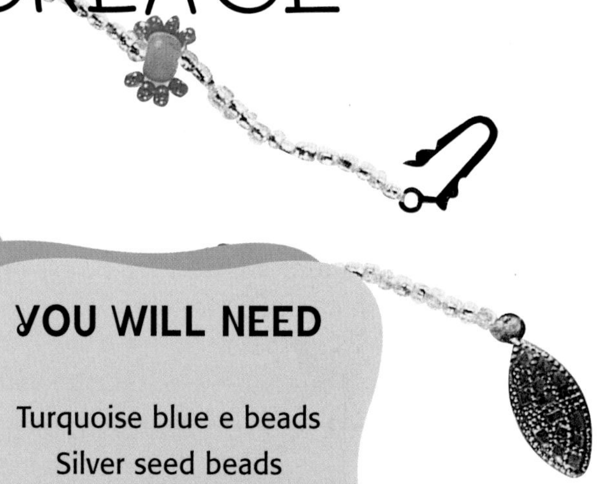

YOU WILL NEED

Turquoise blue e beads
Silver seed beads
Royal blue seed beads
Thread
Clasp

1. Center one end of a clasp on a 36"
   (91 cm) thread. Secure the thread to
   the clasp with a double knot.

2. String 15 silver seed beads (**Fig. 1**).

3. String one blue e bead (**Fig. 2**).

4. Separate the strands and string 4
   royal blue seed beads on one of the
   threads (**Fig. 3**).

5. Loop the thread back around the
   bead and pass it through the
   turquoise blue e bead as shown.

6. Repeat steps 4 and 5 with the other
   thread (**Fig. 4**).

Fig. 1

Fig. 2

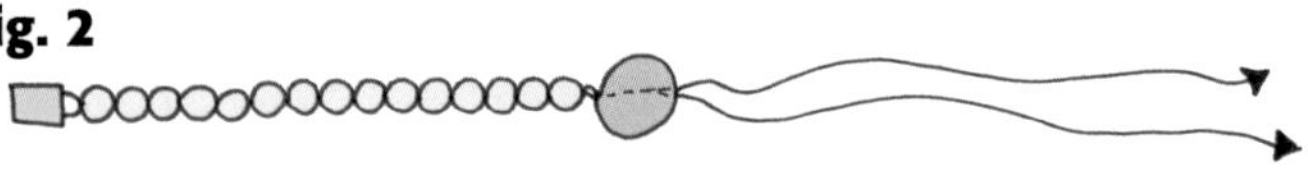

Fig. 3

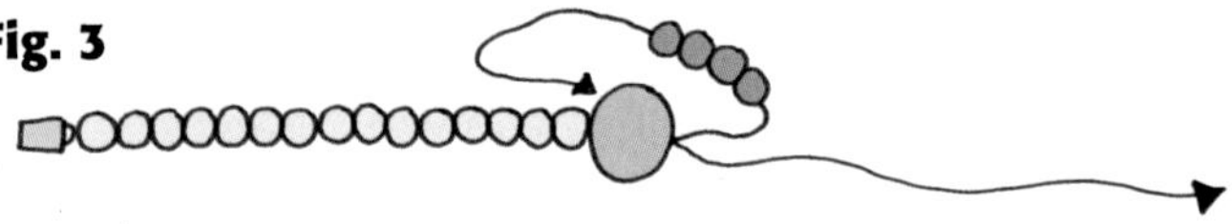

Fig. 4

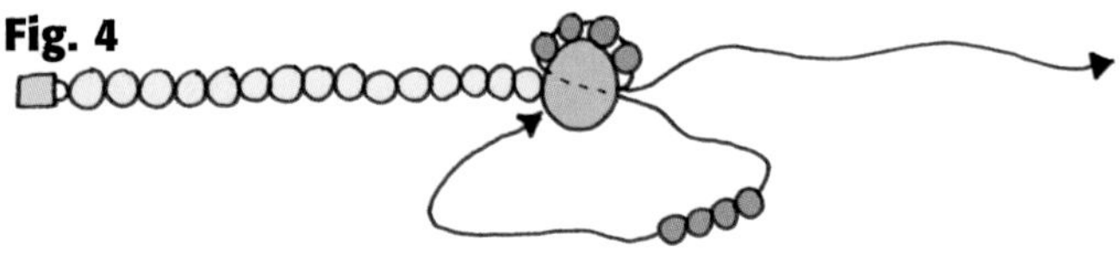

7. Pull tight! (**Fig. 5**).

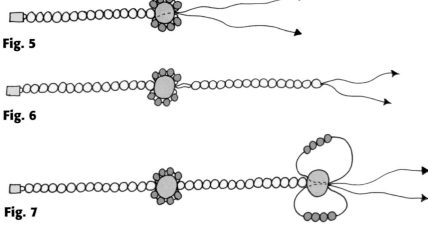

Fig. 5

8. Put the threads together and string 15 silver seed beads (**Fig. 6**).

Fig. 6

9. String a turquoise e bead, add 4 royal blue seed beads to each thread, and pass each thread back through the turquoise blue e bead as you did before (**Fig. 7**).

Fig. 7

10. Remember to pull tight (**Fig. 8**).

Fig. 8

11. Continue the pattern until you have a length that fits comfortably around your neck. Finish by tying the ends to the other end of the clasp and neatening the ends.

TRY THIS
Use 1 mm thick elastic thread and make a strand that fits snugly around your head to make a Sunshine headband. Or make a bracelet to match your necklace, using larger beads.

HANGING LOOPS NECKLACE

TRY THIS
Vary the number and kind of beads you use. Or make a length that fits around your stomach for a belly chain.

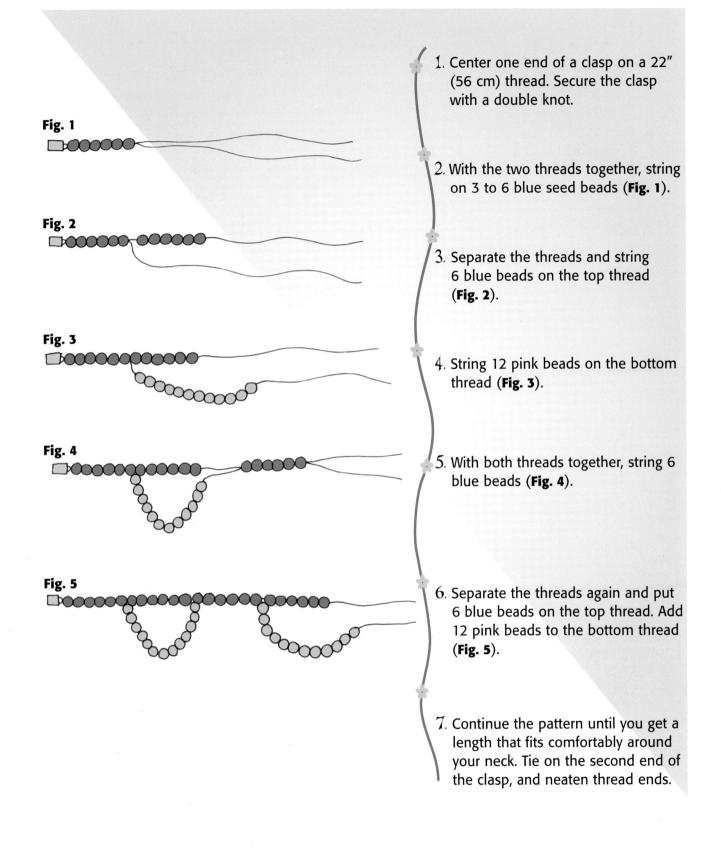

Fig. 1

Fig. 2

Fig. 3

Fig. 4

Fig. 5

1. Center one end of a clasp on a 22″ (56 cm) thread. Secure the clasp with a double knot.

2. With the two threads together, string on 3 to 6 blue seed beads (**Fig. 1**).

3. Separate the threads and string 6 blue beads on the top thread (**Fig. 2**).

4. String 12 pink beads on the bottom thread (**Fig. 3**).

5. With both threads together, string 6 blue beads (**Fig. 4**).

6. Separate the threads again and put 6 blue beads on the top thread. Add 12 pink beads to the bottom thread (**Fig. 5**).

7. Continue the pattern until you get a length that fits comfortably around your neck. Tie on the second end of the clasp, and neaten thread ends.

LINKING **L**OOPS **N**ECKLACE

1. Center one end of a clasp on a 30" (76 cm) thread. Secure the clasp with a double knot.

Fig. 1

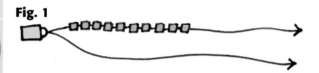

2. Put 10 light purple bugle beads on one strand of the thread (**Fig. 1**).

Fig. 2

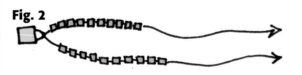

3. Put 10 light purple bugle beads on the other strand of the thread (**Fig. 2**).

Fig. 3

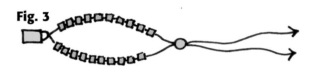

4. Put the two threads together and string both through a green e bead (**Fig. 3**).

Fig. 4

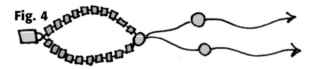

5. Separate the threads and string each through a green e bead (**Fig. 4**).

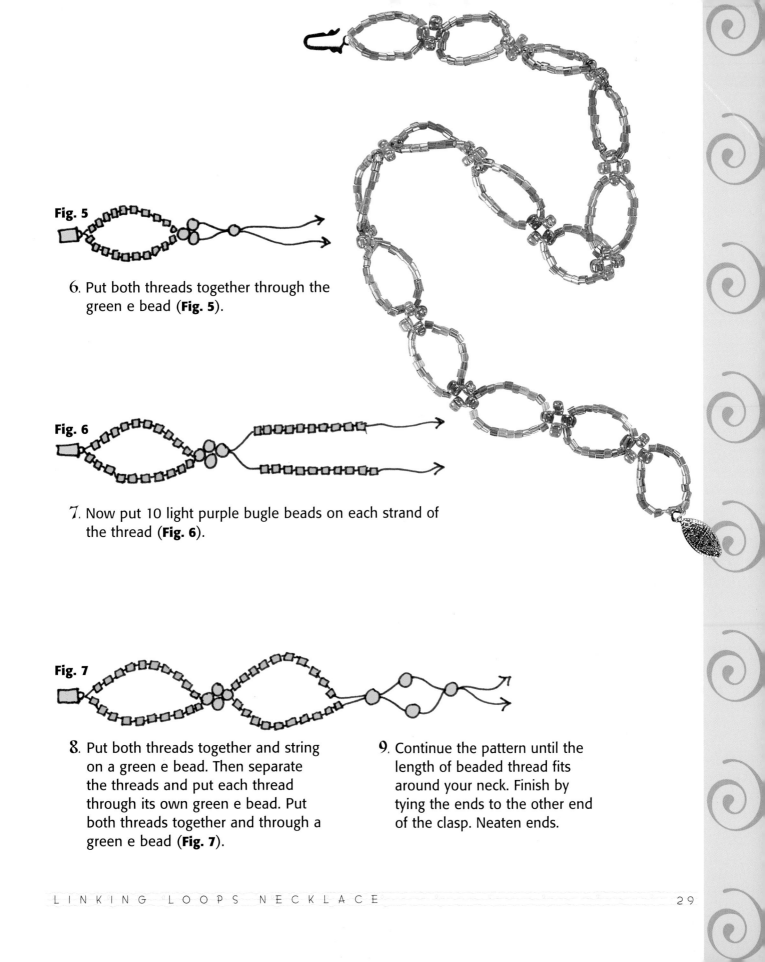

Fig. 5

6. Put both threads together through the green e bead (**Fig. 5**).

Fig. 6

7. Now put 10 light purple bugle beads on each strand of the thread (**Fig. 6**).

Fig. 7

8. Put both threads together and string on a green e bead. Then separate the threads and put each thread through its own green e bead. Put both threads together and through a green e bead (**Fig. 7**).

9. Continue the pattern until the length of beaded thread fits around your neck. Finish by tying the ends to the other end of the clasp. Neaten ends.

ICICLES NECKLACE

1. Tie on one half of a clasp to a single thread 23"
   (58 cm) long. Leave a tail of 2" (5 cm) before
   tying it on. Make a strand of beads with the
   pattern one bugle bead and one seed bead,
   until you get a strand that fits around your neck
   (**Fig. 1**). Make sure the final length has an even
   number of bugle beads and odd number of
   e beads.

2. Finish the strand by tying it to the second end of
   a clasp.

3. Count the number of e beads to find the
   center of the strand and mark it with a
   bit of tape or string.

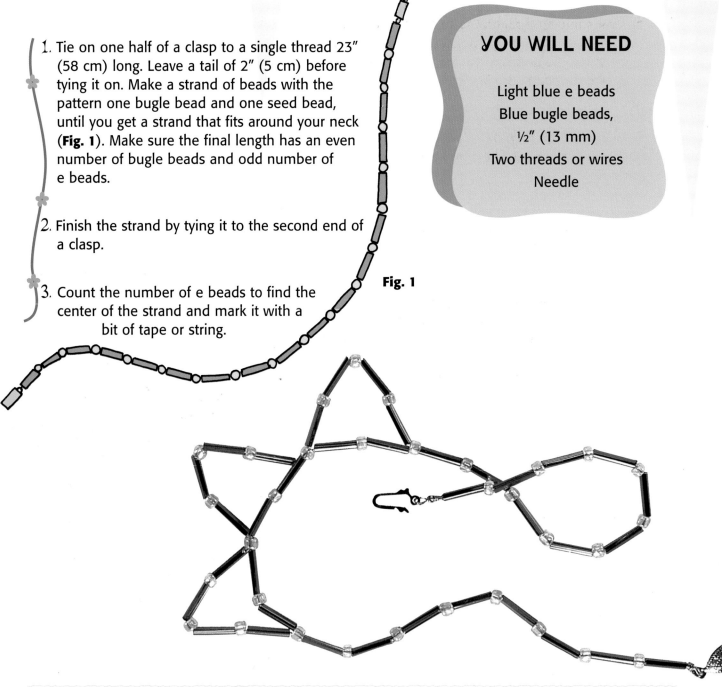

Fig. 1

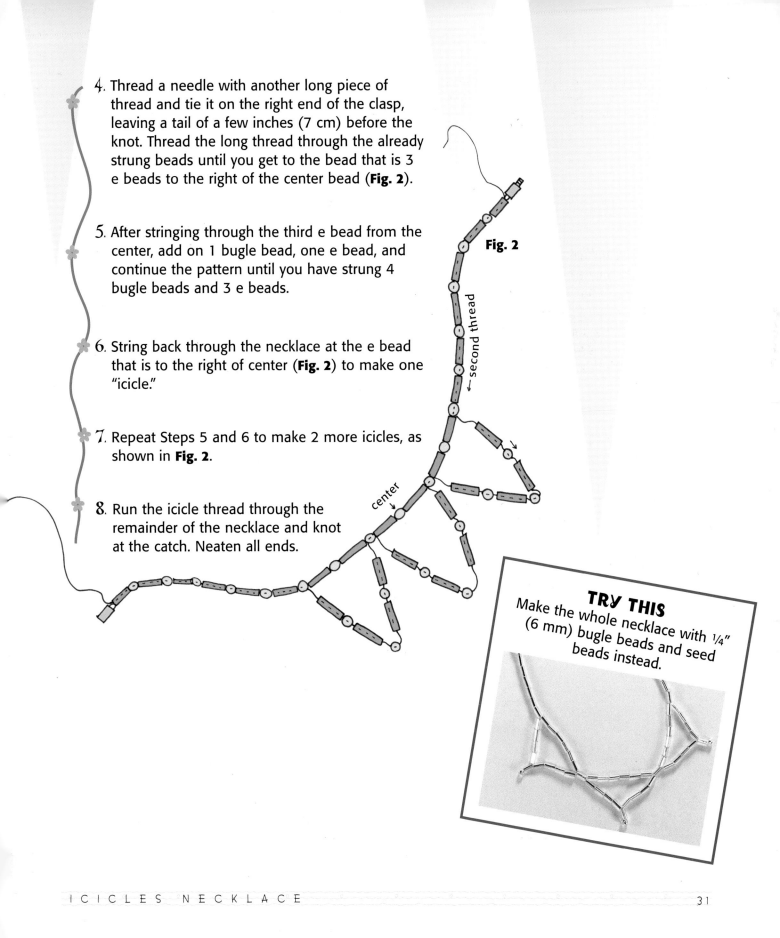

4. Thread a needle with another long piece of thread and tie it on the right end of the clasp, leaving a tail of a few inches (7 cm) before the knot. Thread the long thread through the already strung beads until you get to the bead that is 3 e beads to the right of the center bead (**Fig. 2**).

5. After stringing through the third e bead from the center, add on 1 bugle bead, one e bead, and continue the pattern until you have strung 4 bugle beads and 3 e beads.

6. String back through the necklace at the e bead that is to the right of center (**Fig. 2**) to make one "icicle."

7. Repeat Steps 5 and 6 to make 2 more icicles, as shown in **Fig. 2**.

8. Run the icicle thread through the remainder of the necklace and knot at the catch. Neaten all ends.

Fig. 2

← second thread

center ↓

TRY THIS

Make the whole necklace with ¼" (6 mm) bugle beads and seed beads instead.

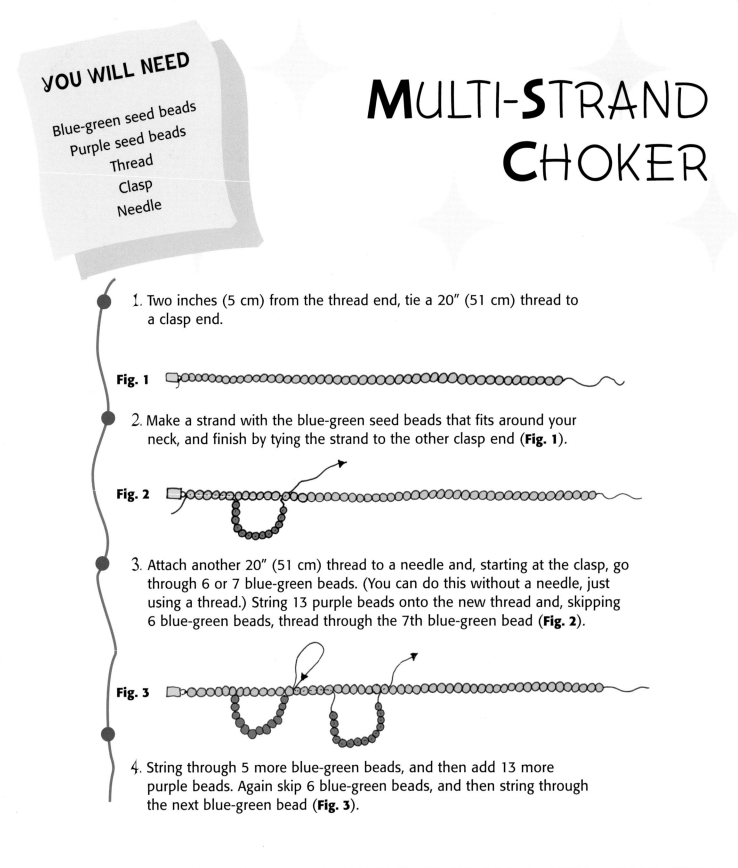

MULTI-STRAND CHOKER

1. Two inches (5 cm) from the thread end, tie a 20" (51 cm) thread to a clasp end.

Fig. 1

2. Make a strand with the blue-green seed beads that fits around your neck, and finish by tying the strand to the other clasp end (**Fig. 1**).

Fig. 2

3. Attach another 20" (51 cm) thread to a needle and, starting at the clasp, go through 6 or 7 blue-green beads. (You can do this without a needle, just using a thread.) String 13 purple beads onto the new thread and, skipping 6 blue-green beads, thread through the 7th blue-green bead (**Fig. 2**).

Fig. 3

4. String through 5 more blue-green beads, and then add 13 more purple beads. Again skip 6 blue-green beads, and then string through the next blue-green bead (**Fig. 3**).

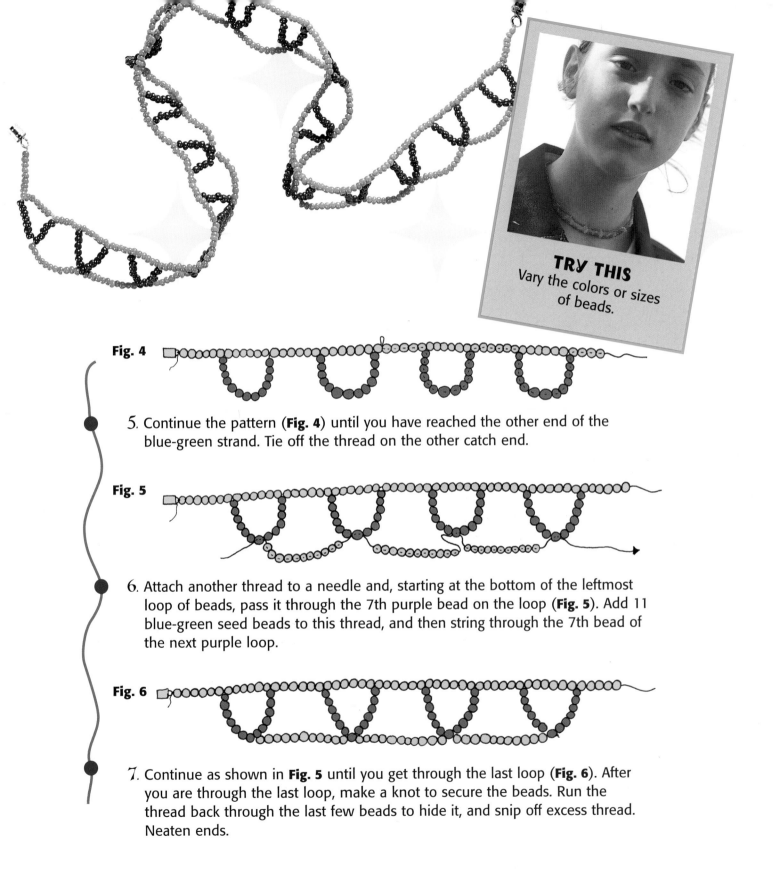

Fig. 4

5. Continue the pattern (**Fig. 4**) until you have reached the other end of the blue-green strand. Tie off the thread on the other catch end.

Fig. 5

6. Attach another thread to a needle and, starting at the bottom of the leftmost loop of beads, pass it through the 7th purple bead on the loop (**Fig. 5**). Add 11 blue-green seed beads to this thread, and then string through the 7th bead of the next purple loop.

Fig. 6

7. Continue as shown in **Fig. 5** until you get through the last loop (**Fig. 6**). After you are through the last loop, make a knot to secure the beads. Run the thread back through the last few beads to hide it, and snip off excess thread. Neaten ends.

Flowers and Leaves Necklace

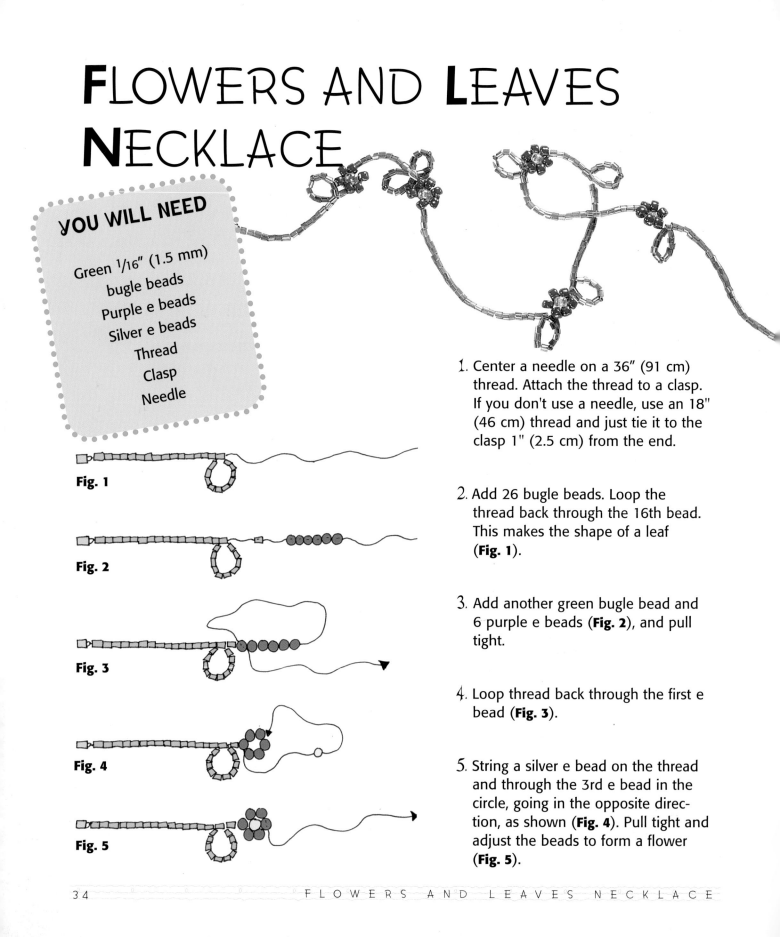

Fig. 1

Fig. 2

Fig. 3

Fig. 4

Fig. 5

1. Center a needle on a 36" (91 cm) thread. Attach the thread to a clasp. If you don't use a needle, use an 18" (46 cm) thread and just tie it to the clasp 1" (2.5 cm) from the end.

2. Add 26 bugle beads. Loop the thread back through the 16th bead. This makes the shape of a leaf (**Fig. 1**).

3. Add another green bugle bead and 6 purple e beads (**Fig. 2**), and pull tight.

4. Loop thread back through the first e bead (**Fig. 3**).

5. String a silver e bead on the thread and through the 3rd e bead in the circle, going in the opposite direction, as shown (**Fig. 4**). Pull tight and adjust the beads to form a flower (**Fig. 5**).

6. Add 10 more bugle beads. Then add 10 more bugle beads and loop back through the 10th bugle bead of the first group as shown in **Fig. 6**. Pull to form a loop.

Fig. 6

7. Add 10 more beads and string back through the same bugle bead you used the last time (**Fig. 7**). Pull to form a loop.

Fig. 7

8. Add 6 purple e beads, and loop back through the first purple e bead (**Fig. 8**).

Fig. 8

9. String a silver e bead on the thread and loop back through the 3rd purple e bead in the opposite direction (**Fig. 9**). Pull tight and adjust beads to make a flower.

Fig. 9

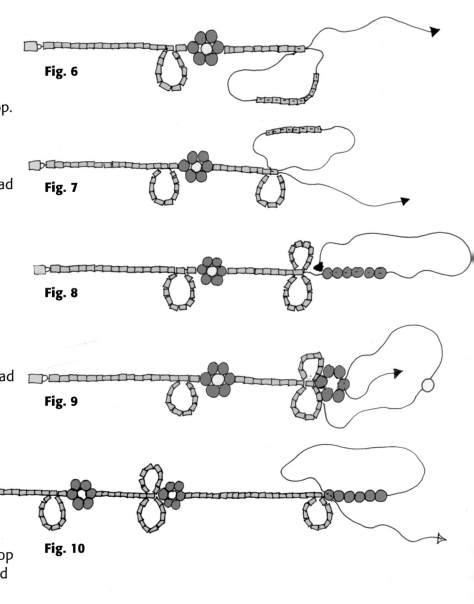

10. Add 20 more green bugle beads. Then add 10 bugle beads and loop back through the 20th bugle bead (**Fig. 10**). Add 6 purple e beads (**Fig. 10**) and a silver e bead to make another flower as you did before.

Fig. 10

11. Add 11 green bugle beads and loop back through the first bugle bead to make a leaf.

12. Continue the pattern of Flowers and Leaves to make a length that fits around your neck, and tie on a clasp end.

FLOWERS OUT OF LINE

YOU WILL NEED

Silver seed beads
Purple seed beads
Thread
Clasp
Needle

This necklace has to be made with an extra-long thread, at least three times the finished length you want.

1. Center a needle on a 6-foot (1.82 m) thread; then tie the thread ends to a clasp end 2" (5 cm) from the end. If you aren't using a needle, use half the length (3 feet or 91 cm), and attach the thread to the clasp. Add 6 purple beads (**Fig. 1**).

2. Loop back through the first of the 6 beads in the direction shown (**Fig. 2**).

3. Pull tight, and then add one silver bead (**Fig. 3**).

4. String back through the 5th bead from the start of the circle in a clockwise direction, as shown (**Fig. 4**). When you do this, the flower will flip over.

5. Pull tight and adjust the beads to make a flower (**Fig. 5**).

6. String 6 silver beads (**Fig. 6**).

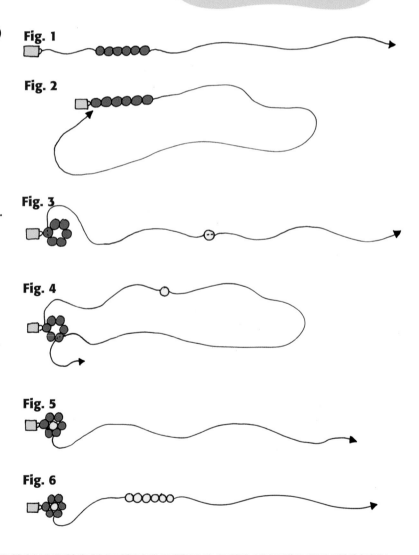

Fig. 1

Fig. 2

Fig. 3

Fig. 4

Fig. 5

Fig. 6

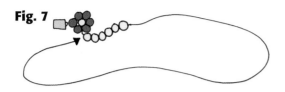

Fig. 7

7. String back through the first of the 6 silver beads to make a circle (**Fig. 7**).

Fig. 8

8. Pull tight, making sure there is no extra space between this bead circle and the first flower (**Fig. 8**). This is especially important for making the Flowers Out of Line.

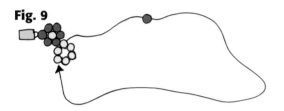

Fig. 9

9. String one purple bead, and then string the thread through the 5th bead in the circle (**Fig. 9**), going clockwise from the start. (Don't worry if the flower flips over. This is right.)

Fig. 10

10. Pull tight and adjust the beads (**Fig. 10**).

11. Continue to make flowers, alternating colors, until you have a length that fits around your neck. Finish by attaching the thread end to the second clasp end. Neaten ends.

BRACELETS AND ANKLETS

ZigZag Flowers Bracelet

YOU WILL NEED

Orange e beads
Magenta e beads
Purple ½" (13 mm)
bugle beads
Thread
Clasp
Needle

1. Center a needle on a 40" (102 cm) thread. Then attach thread ends to a clasp. If you aren't using a needle, use 20" (51 cm) of thread and attach to the clasp 2" (5 cm) from the end.

Fig. 2

3. Pull tight and then add one orange bead (**Fig. 2**).

Fig. 3

Fig. 1

2. Add 6 magenta e beads. Then loop back through the first of the 6 beads in the clockwise direction shown in **Fig. 1**.

4. String back through the 5th bead in the circle, going clockwise as shown in **Fig. 3**. When you do this, the flower will flip over.

Fig. 4

Fig. 5

5. Pull tight and adjust the beads to make a flower. Next string a purple bugle bead (**Fig. 4**).

6. Add 6 magenta beads (**Fig. 5**).

Fig. 6

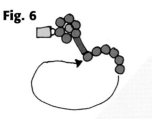

Fig. 7

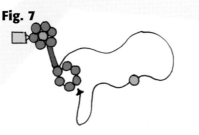

Fig. 8

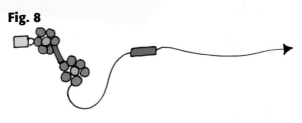

7. Loop back through the first of the 6 magenta beads to make a circle (**Fig. 6**). Pull tight, making sure that there is no extra space between this bead circle and the bugle bead. This is especially important for making the zigzag pattern work.

8. String one orange bead, and then string the thread through the 5th bead in the circle (**Fig. 7**). Don't worry if the flower flips over. This is right.

9. Pull tight and adjust the beads; then add a purple bugle bead (**Fig. 8**).

TRY THIS
Vary the pattern by using seed beads instead of bugle beads.

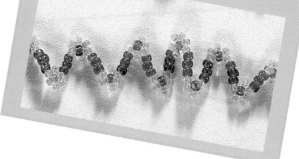

Fig. 9

10. String on 6 magenta beads to start the next circle (**Fig. 9**).

Fig. 10

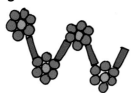

11. Continue the pattern until you have a length that fits around your wrist (**Fig. 10**). Finish by attaching the thread to the other end of the clasp. Neaten ends.

CROSSING STRANDS BRACELET

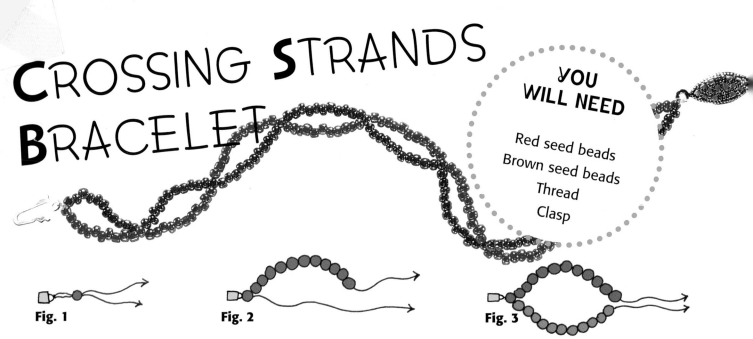

YOU WILL NEED

Red seed beads
Brown seed beads
Thread
Clasp

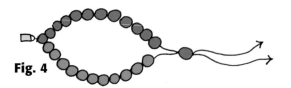

Fig. 1

Fig. 2

Fig. 3

1. Center one end of a clasp on a 22" (56 cm) thread. Secure the clasp with a double knot. String one brown bead on both threads (**Fig. 1**).

2. Separate the threads and add 11 brown beads to one thread (**Fig. 2**).

3. Add 11 red seed beads to the other thread (**Fig. 3**).

Fig. 4

Fig. 5

4. Put the threads together and string one brown bead (**Fig. 4**).

5. Add 11 brown beads to the bottom thread (**Fig. 5**).

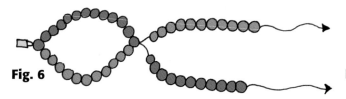

Fig. 6

Fig. 7

6. Add 11 red beads to the top thread (**Fig. 6**).

7. Put the threads together, and string a brown bead (**Fig. 7**).

8. Continue the pattern until you get a length that fits around your wrist. Finish by attaching the thread ends to the other side of the clasp. Neaten ends.

COILED SNAKE BRACELET

Fig. 1

Fig. 2

Fig. 3

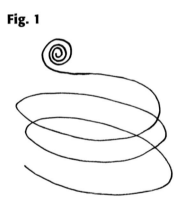

Fig. 4

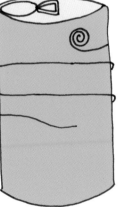

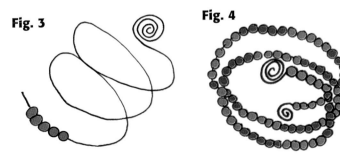

1. Use the long-nose pliers to curl in one end of the wire like a snail, as shown in **Fig. 1**.

2. Wrap the rest of the wire around the can to make the coiled shape (**Fig. 2**). Remove from can.

3. Add 5 black e beads on the wire (**Fig. 3**), and then 5 dark brown beads. Continue this pattern until you fill the wire, but leave enough wire for another curl at the end.

4. Use the long-nose pliers to curl in the second wire end in the same way you did the first end (**Fig. 4**).

5. Try on the bracelet. Make the coil tighter or looser to make it fit around your wrist. This piece also can be worn as a necklace or armband.

CHAIN OF FLOWERS BRACELET

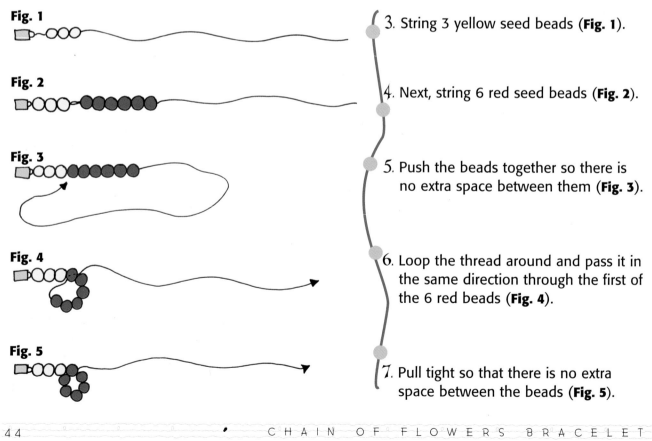

YOU WILL NEED

Yellow seed beads
Red seed beads
Thread
Clasp
Needle

1. For making flowers, use a length of thread 3 times the length you would like your finished project to be. This project uses a lot of thread!

2. String a needle on a doubled 36" (91 cm) thread and tie the thread at its center to one end of a clasp. If you aren't using a needle, use 18" (46 cm) of thread, and 2" (5 cm) from the thread end, tie the thread to one end of the clasp.

Fig. 1

3. String 3 yellow seed beads (**Fig. 1**).

Fig. 2

4. Next, string 6 red seed beads (**Fig. 2**).

Fig. 3

5. Push the beads together so there is no extra space between them (**Fig. 3**).

Fig. 4

6. Loop the thread around and pass it in the same direction through the first of the 6 red beads (**Fig. 4**).

Fig. 5

7. Pull tight so that there is no extra space between the beads (**Fig. 5**).

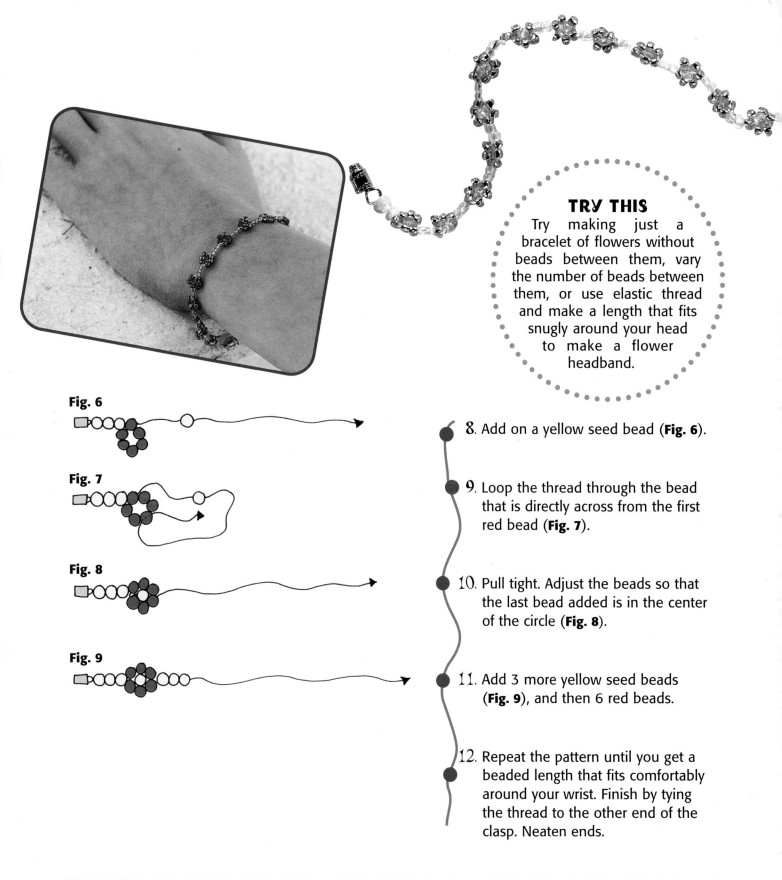

TRY THIS
Try making just a bracelet of flowers without beads between them, vary the number of beads between them, or use elastic thread and make a length that fits snugly around your head to make a flower headband.

Fig. 6

Fig. 7

Fig. 8

Fig. 9

8. Add on a yellow seed bead (**Fig. 6**).

9. Loop the thread through the bead that is directly across from the first red bead (**Fig. 7**).

10. Pull tight. Adjust the beads so that the last bead added is in the center of the circle (**Fig. 8**).

11. Add 3 more yellow seed beads (**Fig. 9**), and then 6 red beads.

12. Repeat the pattern until you get a beaded length that fits comfortably around your wrist. Finish by tying the thread to the other end of the clasp. Neaten ends.

SQUARES BRACELET

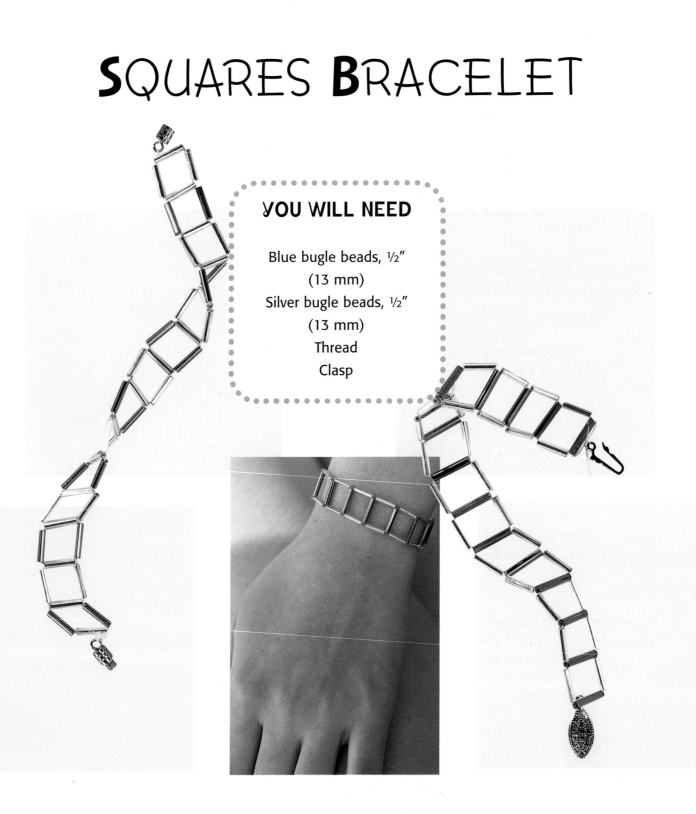

1. Center one end of a clasp on a 22″ (56 cm) thread. Secure the clasp with a double knot. Add a blue bugle bead to one of the two threads (**Fig. 1**).

2. String the other thread through the same blue bugle bead in the opposite direction, as shown in **Fig. 2**.

3. Add a silver bugle bead to each of the two threads (**Fig. 3**).

4. String another blue bugle bead on one thread (**Fig. 4**).

5. String the other thread through the same blue bugle bead in the opposite direction (**Fig. 5**).

6. Pull tight to make sure there is no extra space between beads (**Fig. 6**).

7. Continue the pattern (**Fig. 7**) until you get a length that fits around your wrist. Finish by attaching the other end of the clasp. Neaten ends.

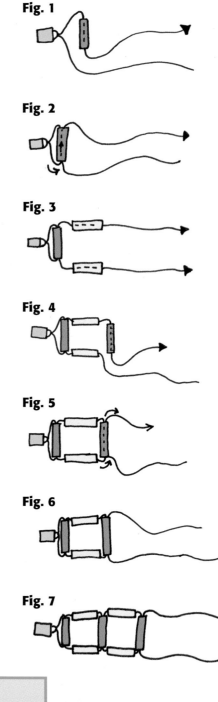

Fig. 1

Fig. 2

Fig. 3

Fig. 4

Fig. 5

Fig. 6

Fig. 7

TRY THIS
Use elastic thread and make the strand long enough to fit around your head to make a squares headband.

DIAMONDS BRACELET

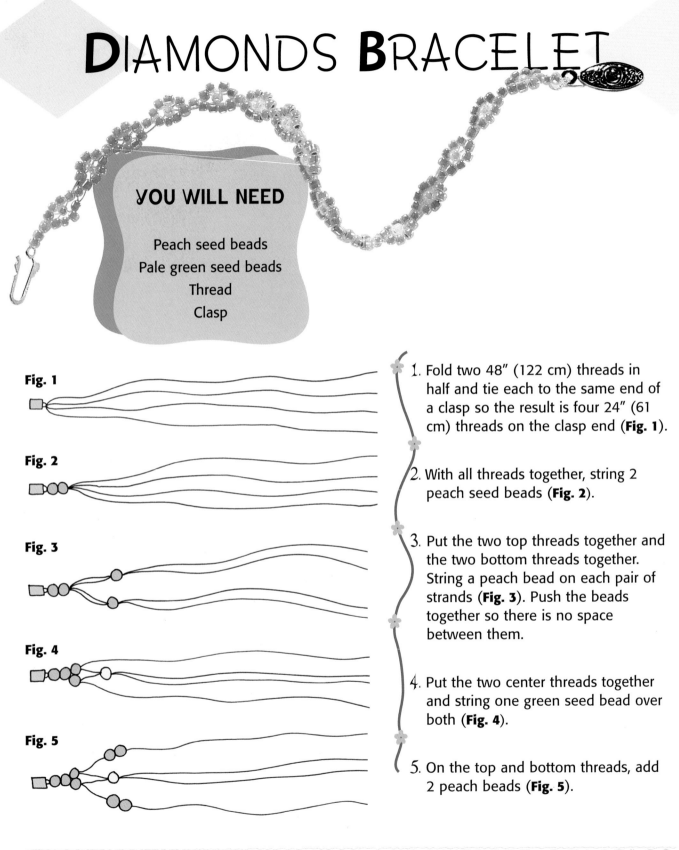

YOU WILL NEED

Peach seed beads
Pale green seed beads
Thread
Clasp

Fig. 1

Fig. 2

Fig. 3

Fig. 4

Fig. 5

1. Fold two 48" (122 cm) threads in half and tie each to the same end of a clasp so the result is four 24" (61 cm) threads on the clasp end (**Fig. 1**).

2. With all threads together, string 2 peach seed beads (**Fig. 2**).

3. Put the two top threads together and the two bottom threads together. String a peach bead on each pair of strands (**Fig. 3**). Push the beads together so there is no space between them.

4. Put the two center threads together and string one green seed bead over both (**Fig. 4**).

5. On the top and bottom threads, add 2 peach beads (**Fig. 5**).

6. Push the beads together. Then pair the two top threads and two bottom threads. String a peach bead on each pair of threads (**Fig. 6**).

7. Put the two middle threads together and string one peach bead (**Fig. 7**). Put the top two threads and the bottom two threads together and string one peach bead on each (**Fig. 7**).

Fig. 6

Fig. 7

8. Separate the top and bottom threads, and add two peach beads to each (**Fig. 8**). Put the two center threads together and string a green bead (**Fig. 8**).

Fig. 8

9. Put the top two and bottom two threads together and add a peach bead to each (**Fig. 9**).

Fig. 9

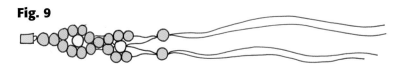

10. Push the beads together so there is no extra space between them (**Fig. 10**), and continue the pattern until you get a length that fits around your wrist. Attach the threads to the other end of the clasp. Neaten ends.

Fig. 10

TRIANGLES BRACELET

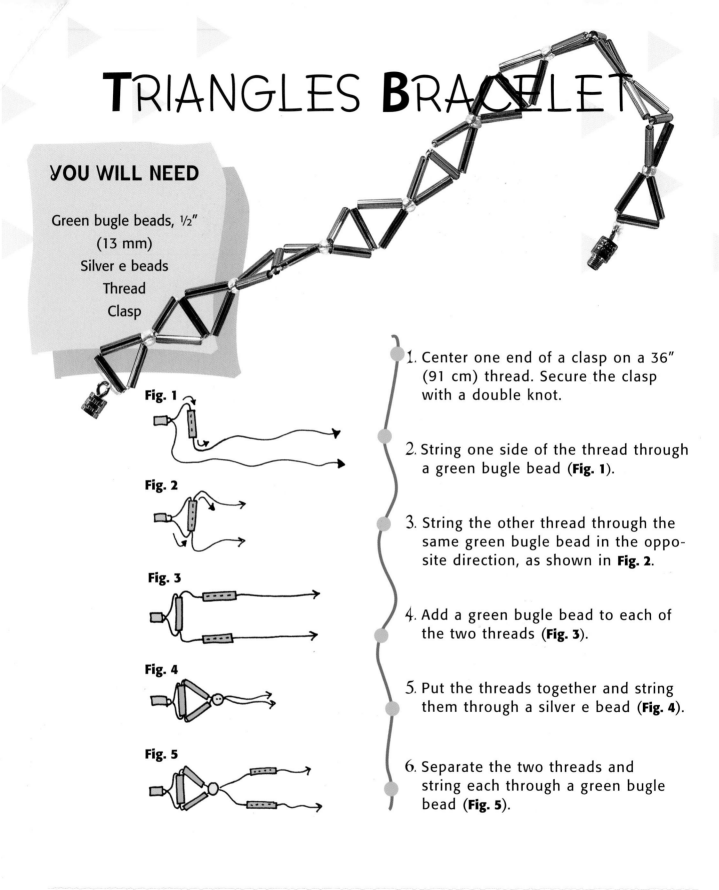

YOU WILL NEED

Green bugle beads, ½"
(13 mm)
Silver e beads
Thread
Clasp

Fig. 1

Fig. 2

Fig. 3

Fig. 4

Fig. 5

1. Center one end of a clasp on a 36"
   (91 cm) thread. Secure the clasp
   with a double knot.

2. String one side of the thread through
   a green bugle bead (**Fig. 1**).

3. String the other thread through the
   same green bugle bead in the opposite direction, as shown in **Fig. 2**.

4. Add a green bugle bead to each of
   the two threads (**Fig. 3**).

5. Put the threads together and string
   them through a silver e bead (**Fig. 4**).

6. Separate the two threads and
   string each through a green bugle
   bead (**Fig. 5**).

7. Add another bugle bead on one of the threads (**Fig. 6**).

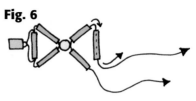

Fig. 6

8. String the other thread back through the latest bugle bead in the opposite direction (**Fig. 7**). Pull tight so the beads are all close together and there is no extra space between the beads.

Fig. 7

9. Add a bugle bead to each of the threads (**Fig. 8**).

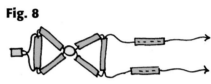

Fig. 8

10. Put the threads together and add a silver e bead (**Fig. 9**).

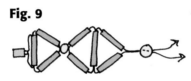

Fig. 9

11. Continue the pattern until you get a length that fits around your wrist. Finish by tying the threads to the other end of the clasp. Neaten ends.

TRY THIS
Make matching triangles earrings.

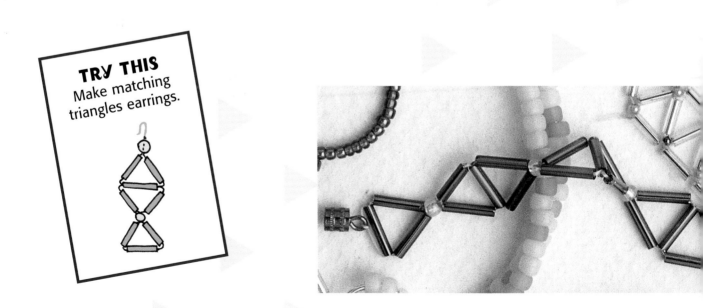

TECHNO TRIANGLES BRACELET

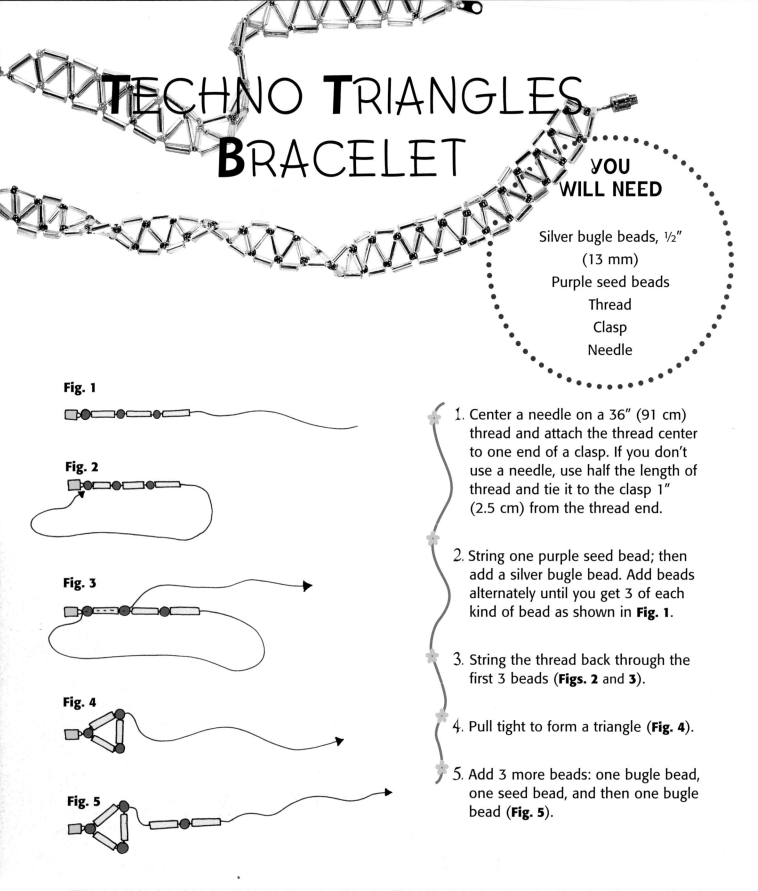

YOU WILL NEED

Silver bugle beads, ½"
(13 mm)
Purple seed beads
Thread
Clasp
Needle

Fig. 1

Fig. 2

Fig. 3

Fig. 4

Fig. 5

1. Center a needle on a 36" (91 cm) thread and attach the thread center to one end of a clasp. If you don't use a needle, use half the length of thread and tie it to the clasp 1" (2.5 cm) from the thread end.

2. String one purple seed bead; then add a silver bugle bead. Add beads alternately until you get 3 of each kind of bead as shown in **Fig. 1**.

3. String the thread back through the first 3 beads (**Figs. 2** and **3**).

4. Pull tight to form a triangle (**Fig. 4**).

5. Add 3 more beads: one bugle bead, one seed bead, and then one bugle bead (**Fig. 5**).

Fig. 6

Fig. 7

Fig. 8

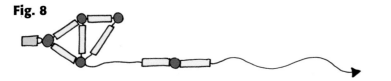

Fig. 9

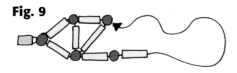

Fig. 10

Fig. 11

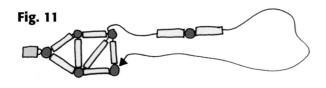

Fig. 12

6. String back through the bottom seed bead of the first triangle, as shown in **Figs. 6** and **7**.

7. Add 3 more beads: one bugle bead, one seed bead, and then one bugle bead (**Fig. 8**).

8. String back though the top seed bead, as shown (**Fig. 9**), and pull tight (**Fig. 10**).

9. Continue the pattern (**Figs. 11** and **12**) until you get a length that fits around your wrist. Tie the threads to the second end of the clasp. Neaten ends.

WAVES AND PEARLS ANKLET

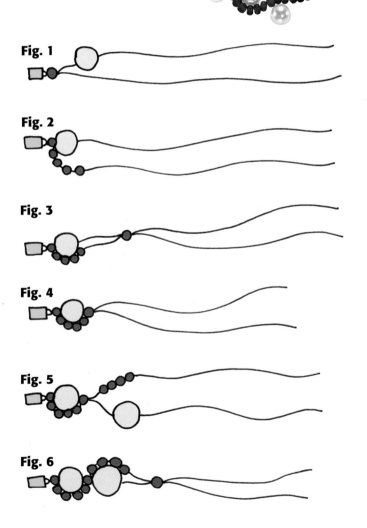

1. Center one end of a clasp on a 24″ (61 cm) thread. Secure the clasp with a double knot. String one purple e bead onto both thread ends. Separate the threads and add a pearl to the top thread (**Fig. 1**).

2. Add 4 purple e beads to the bottom strand (**Fig. 2**).

3. Put both threads together and add on purple e bead (**Fig. 3**).

4. Push the beads close together so there is no space in between (**Fig. 4**).

5. Add 4 purple e beads to the top thread. Add one pearl to the bottom thread (**Fig. 5**).

6. Put both threads together and add one purple e bead (**Fig. 6**).

Fig. 1

Fig. 2

Fig. 3

Fig. 4

Fig. 5

Fig. 6

YOU WILL NEED

Pearls
Purple e beads
Thread
Clasp

7. Again, pull really hard so there is no extra space and the beads are right up against each other (**Fig. 7**).

Fig. 7

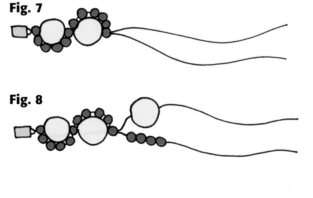

8. Add one pearl on the top thread and 4 purple e beads on the bottom thread (**Fig. 8**).

Fig. 8

9. Add one purple e bead on both threads together (**Fig. 9**).

Fig. 9

10. Continue this pattern until the length fits around your ankle. Tie the threads to the other end of the clasp. Neaten ends.

HANGING CIRCLES ANKLET

YOU WILL NEED

Red seed beads

Light purple seed beads

Thread

Clasp

Needle (optional)

1. Attach one end of a 23" (58 cm) thread to one end of a clasp, 2" (5 cm) from the end. String 10 to 15 purple seed beads on the thread (**Fig. 1**).

Fig. 1

2. Next string 6 red seed beads (**Fig. 2**). Push the beads together so there is no extra space between them.

Fig. 2

HANGING CIRCLES ANKLET

3. Loop the string back through the first of the 6 red seed beads (**Fig. 3**).

Fig. 3

4. Add 15 more purple seed beads (**Fig. 4**).

Fig. 4

5. String 6 more red seed beads and loop the string back through the first of the 6 red seed beads (**Fig. 5**).

Fig. 5

6. Continue the pattern until you get a length that fits comfortably around your ankle. Tie on the other end of the clasp. Neaten ends.

TRY THIS

Use elastic thread and make a short length of beads that fits around your finger for a beaded ring.

HAIR ORNAMENTS

BRAIDED HEADBAND

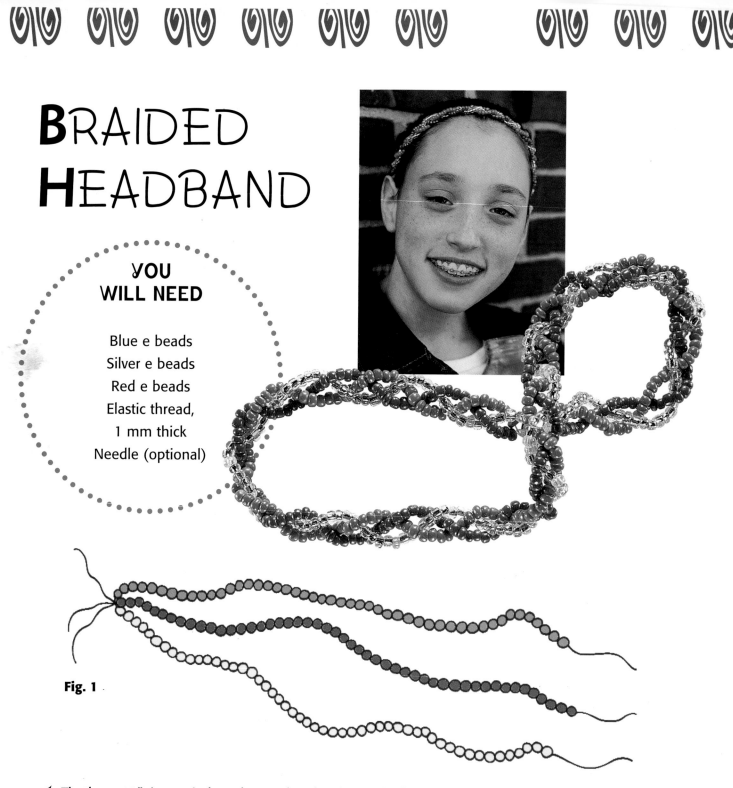

Blue e beads
Silver e beads
Red e beads
Elastic thread,
1 mm thick
Needle (optional)

Fig. 1

1. Tie three 18" (46 cm) threads together, leaving an inch (2.5 cm) before the knot. Add e beads to each of the strands: blue beads on the first, red on the second, and silver on the third. Add beads until you get a length that fits around your head (**Fig. 1**). Take away about 10 beads—the band has to be a little snug so that it can stretch to fit on your head.

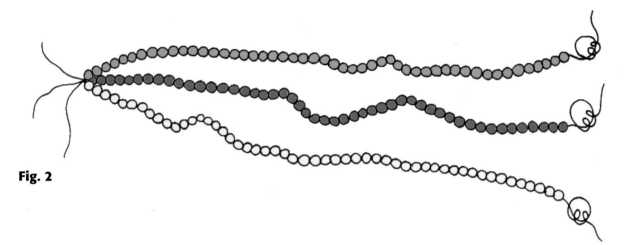

Fig. 2

2. At the end of each strand, tie a knot (**Fig. 2**).

Fig. 3

3. Braid the three strands together (**Fig. 3**).

4. Tie the three strands together after braiding, and then tie the beginning and ending thread tails together to make a circle. Trim off the excess threads.

YOU WILL NEED

Black e beads

Clear e beads

Elastic thread, 1 mm thick

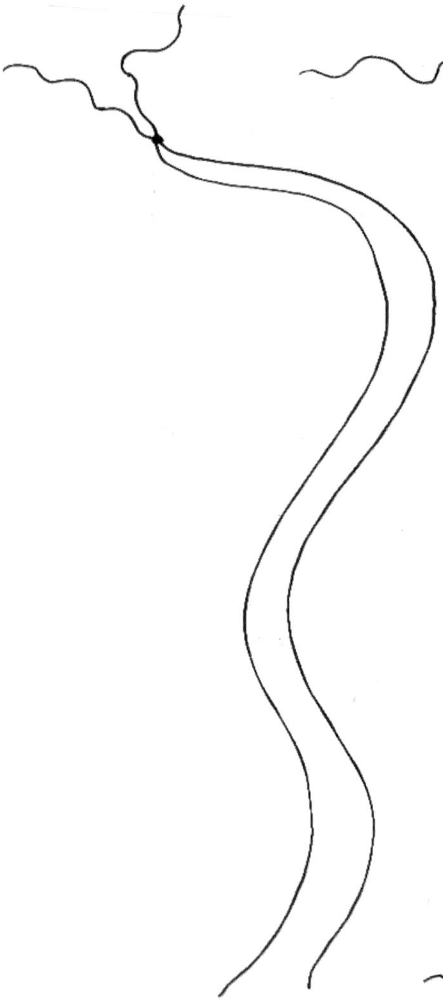

ROMAN HEADBAND

1. Tie two pieces of 18" (46 cm) elastic thread together, 2" from the ends (**Fig. 1**).

2. String beads on one thread, alternating two black e beads and two clear e beads. Keep adding beads until you get a length that fits snugly around your head. Check to make sure that the headband fits well; take away or add beads as needed.

3. String beads on the second thread as for the first thread, making a strand of beads the same length as the first strand (**Fig. 2**).

4. Tie the two threads together at the ends; then tie the start and end of the two threads together to make a circle.

5. When you wear this headband, separate the two strands, leaving a space in between to wear it like a Roman headband. Push the strands together for a different look.

Fig. 1

Fig. 2

TWISTER **B**ARRETTE

YOU WILL NEED

Blue e beads
Purple e beads
Thread for beading
Barrette (hair clasp) with
holes at ends
Clear thin thread
for wrapping

1. Center a barrette on a 22" (56 cm) thread. Secure the thread to the barrette with a double knot. On one thread end, add purple e beads to run beyond the length of the barrette. You will lose some length when the strands are twisted. On the other thread, add blue e beads to the same length as the purple beads (**Fig. 1**).

2. Tie the ends of the purple bead thread and the blue bead thread together (**Fig. 2**).

3. Twist the two strands a few times. Tie the strands to the second end of the barrette (**Fig. 3**).

4. Tie a thin, clear thread to one barrette end and circle around the barrette top with thread to keep the beads in place (**Fig. 4**). Be sure to open the barrette first, so you don't circle the entire barrette, which would keep it from opening.

Fig. 1

Fig. 2

Fig. 3

Fig. 4

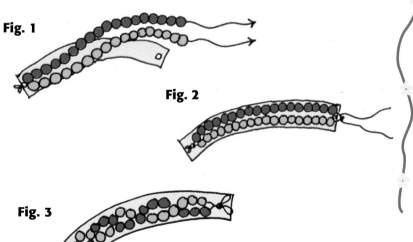

BUGLE BEAD STRIPES BARRETTE

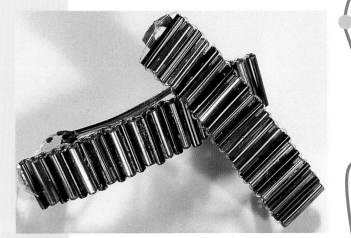

1. Leaving 2" (5 cm) of thread, knot two 10" (25 cm) threads together. String a green bugle bead on one of the threads (**Fig. 1**).

2. Pass the other thread through the same green bugle bead in the opposite direction, as shown in **Fig. 2**, and pull tight.

3. String a pink bugle bead on one of the threads (**Fig. 3**).

4. String the other thread through the pink bugle bead in the opposite direction (**Fig. 4**).

5. Add another green bugle bead (**Fig. 5**) the same way. Continue adding bugle beads in this manner until your beaded strand is the length of the barrette. Tie the ends of the two threads together (**Fig. 6**).

6. Tie each end of the beaded row to the barrette to secure (**Fig. 7**). If you are using a barrette that doesn't have holes, glue the beaded row to the barrette.

Fig. 1

Fig. 2

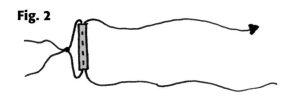

Fig. 3

Fig. 4

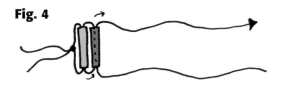

Fig. 5

Fig. 6

Fig. 7

TRY THIS
String the beads lengthwise for another pattern (see photo). Or use the main pattern but make a length of stripes that just fits around your neck, for a choker. Add catches or sew onto a ribbon.

FESTIVE STRIPES BARRETTE

YOU WILL NEED

Green e beads
Silver e beads
Barrette (hair clasp)
Thread
Glue

Fig. 1

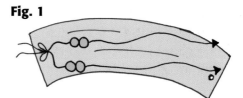

1. Fold a 30" (76 cm) thread in half and put the folded end through a hole at one end of a barrette. Tie the folded end to the barrette with a double knot. (If you are using a barrette that doesn't have holes, just make a knot in the thread center and continue.) On each of the strands, add two green e beads (**Fig. 1**).

Fig. 2

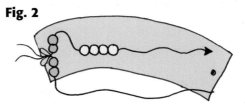

2. On one of the strands, add 4 silver e beads (**Fig. 2**).

Fig. 3

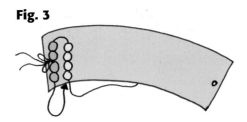

3. String the other strand through the 4 silver e beads in the opposite direction, as shown in **Fig. 3**.

4. Pull tight to make sure that there is no extra space between beads (**Fig. 4**).

5. Add 4 green e beads on one strand (**Fig. 5**).

6. String the other strand through these 4 green e beads, going in the opposite direction (**Fig. 6**).

7. Pull tight (**Fig. 7**).

8. Add enough beads to cover the length of the barrette. Tie the thread ends together. Then put a little glue on the barrette and press the beads down until the glue dries (**Fig. 8**).

9. Tie the loose thread ends to the barrette.

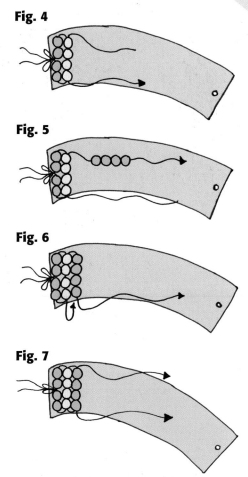

Fig. 4

Fig. 5

Fig. 6

Fig. 7

Fig. 8

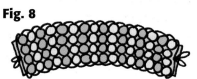

TRY THIS
Use the Festive Stripes pattern, but make a length that just fits around your neck for a choker. Add a clasp or ribbon on the back to wear.

BEADED BOBBY PIN

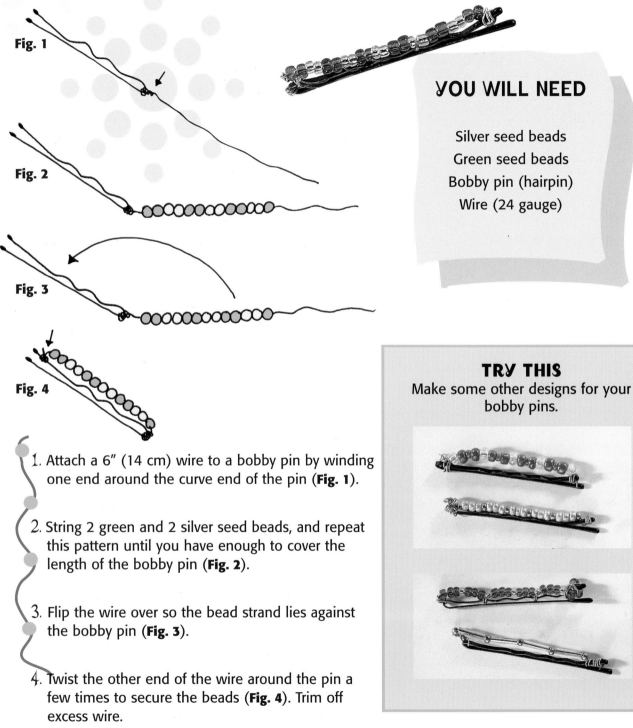

Fig. 1

Fig. 2

Fig. 3

Fig. 4

YOU WILL NEED

Silver seed beads
Green seed beads
Bobby pin (hairpin)
Wire (24 gauge)

TRY THIS
Make some other designs for your
bobby pins.

1. Attach a 6" (14 cm) wire to a bobby pin by winding one end around the curve end of the pin (**Fig. 1**).

2. String 2 green and 2 silver seed beads, and repeat this pattern until you have enough to cover the length of the bobby pin (**Fig. 2**).

3. Flip the wire over so the bead strand lies against the bobby pin (**Fig. 3**).

4. Twist the other end of the wire around the pin a few times to secure the beads (**Fig. 4**). Trim off excess wire.

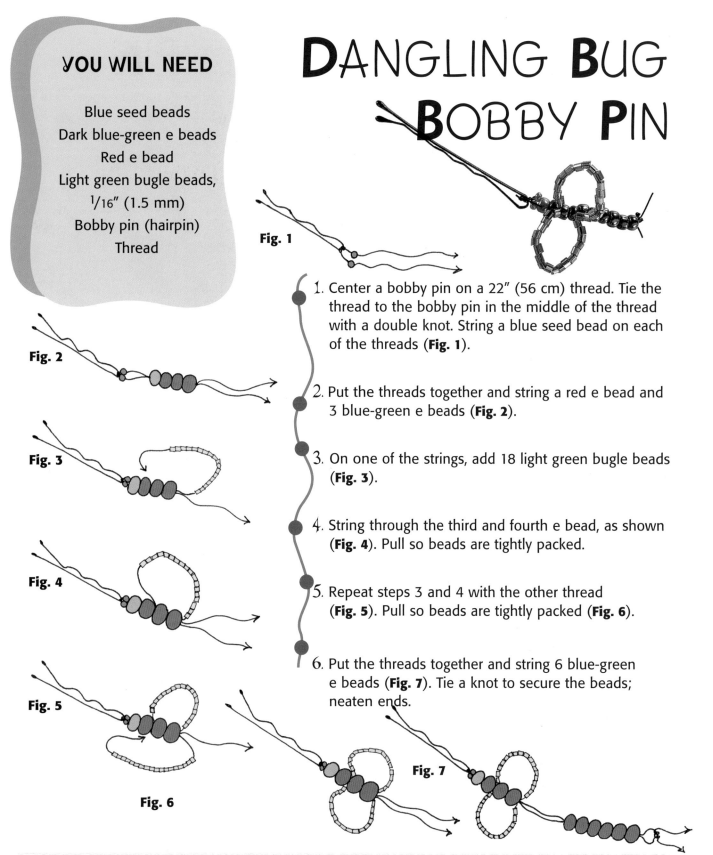

DANGLING BUG BOBBY PIN

YOU WILL NEED

Blue seed beads
Dark blue-green e beads
Red e bead
Light green bugle beads,
$^1/_{16}$" (1.5 mm)
Bobby pin (hairpin)
Thread

Fig. 1

Fig. 2

Fig. 3

Fig. 4

Fig. 5

Fig. 6

Fig. 7

1. Center a bobby pin on a 22" (56 cm) thread. Tie the thread to the bobby pin in the middle of the thread with a double knot. String a blue seed bead on each of the threads (**Fig. 1**).

2. Put the threads together and string a red e bead and 3 blue-green e beads (**Fig. 2**).

3. On one of the strings, add 18 light green bugle beads (**Fig. 3**).

4. String through the third and fourth e bead, as shown (**Fig. 4**). Pull so beads are tightly packed.

5. Repeat steps 3 and 4 with the other thread (**Fig. 5**). Pull so beads are tightly packed (**Fig. 6**).

6. Put the threads together and string 6 blue-green e beads (**Fig. 7**). Tie a knot to secure the beads; neaten ends.

DANGLING BEADS BOBBY PIN

YOU WILL NEED

Green seed beads
Brown seed beads
Bobby pin (hairpin)
Thread

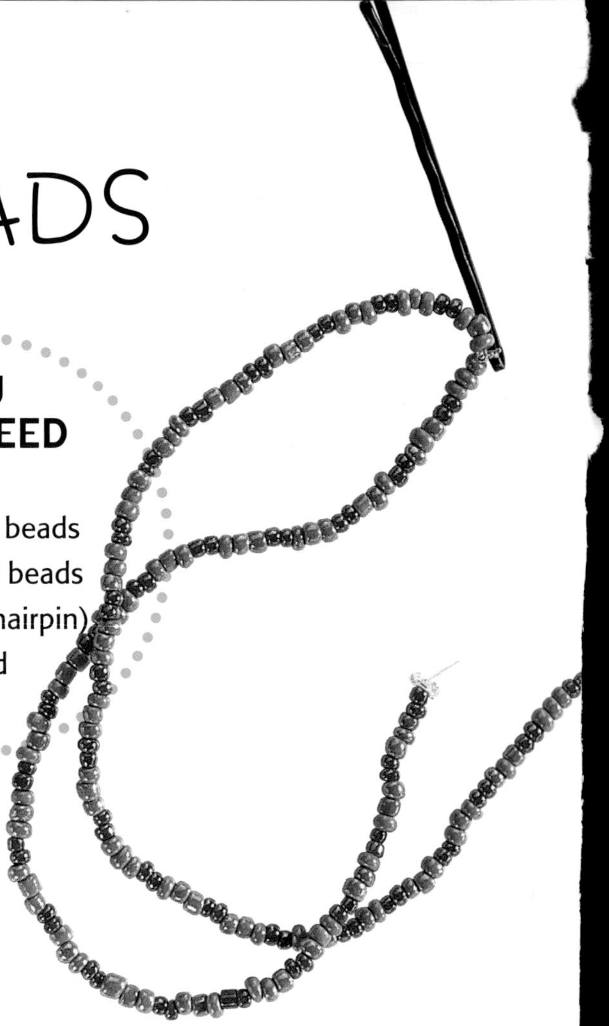

1. Center a bobby pin on a 10″ (25 cm) thread. Secure thread to the pin with a double knot at the curve (**Fig. 1**).

2. On one thread, string 3 green seed beads and 2 brown beads. Repeat this pattern and keep adding beads until your strand is 6″ (15 cm) long, or as long as you like. Repeat on the other thread (**Fig. 2**). Make a knot at the end of each thread to secure the beads.

3. Trim off the ends of thread to finish (**Fig. 3**).

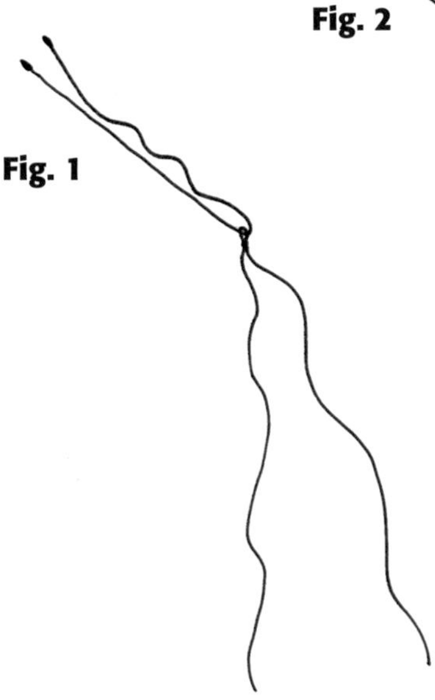

Fig. 1

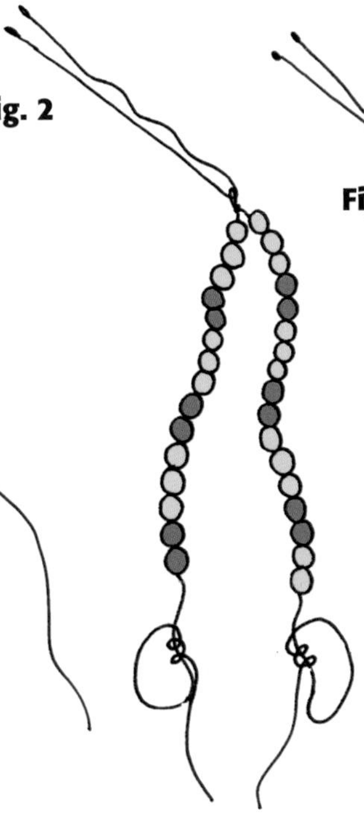

Fig. 2

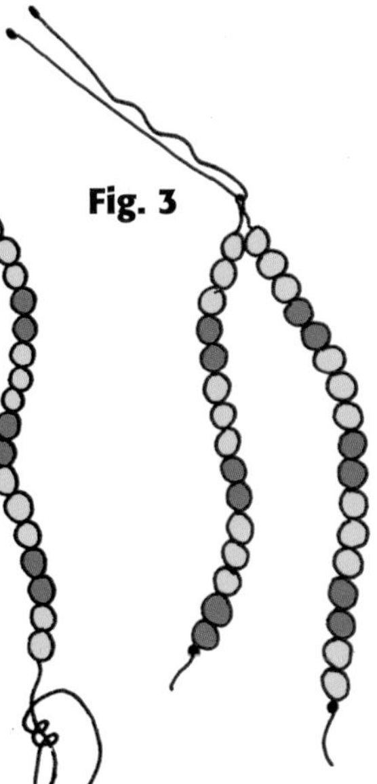

Fig. 3

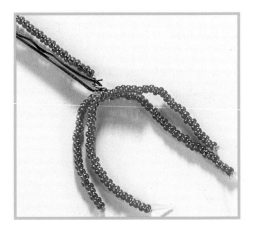

TRY THIS

Lengthen or shorten the strands, or use one of the other bead patterns you have learned to make a fancy bobby pin.

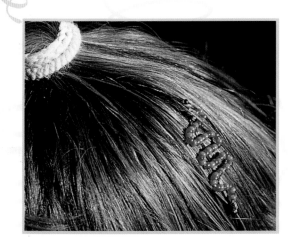

SQUIGGLES BOBBY PIN

YOU WILL NEED

Orange seed beads
Red seed beads
Bobby pin (hairpin)
Wire (24 gauge)

1. Twist one end of a 10" (25 cm) wire to the curve end of a bobby pin. Add orange and red seed beads alternately until you have a strand 3 times as long as the bobby pin (**Fig. 1**).

2. Bend the wire to make squiggles, as shown, and flip the beaded wire over onto the bobby pin.

3. Twist the end of the wire at the opening end of the bobby pin to secure the bead squiggle (**Fig. 3**).

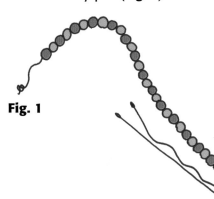

Fig. 1

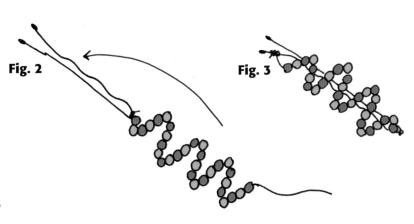

Fig. 2

Fig. 3

HANGING WIRE STAR BOBBY PIN

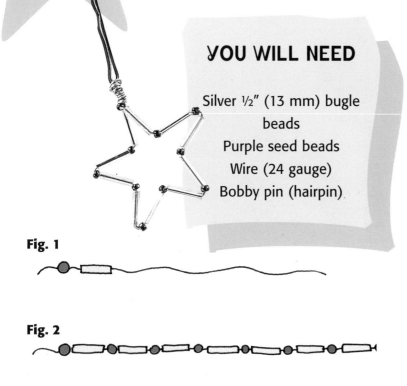

YOU WILL NEED

Silver ½" (13 mm) bugle
beads
Purple seed beads
Wire (24 gauge)
Bobby pin (hairpin)

Fig. 1

Fig. 2

Fig. 3

Fig. 4

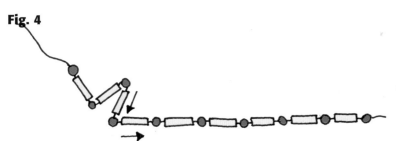

1. On a wire that is 18" long (46 cm),
   string one purple seed bead and
   one silver bugle bead (**Fig. 1**).

2. Continue stringing one purple seed
   bead and then one silver bugle bead
   until you get a total of 10 seed
   beads and 9 bugle beads (**Fig. 2**).

3. Push the beads close together so
   there is no extra space between
   them and there is at least 1" (2.5
   cm) of empty wire at the start and
   at the end. Bend the wire as shown
   (**Fig. 3**) to make a star point (**Fig. 3**).

4. Repeat (**Fig. 4**) until you get the
   shape of the star.

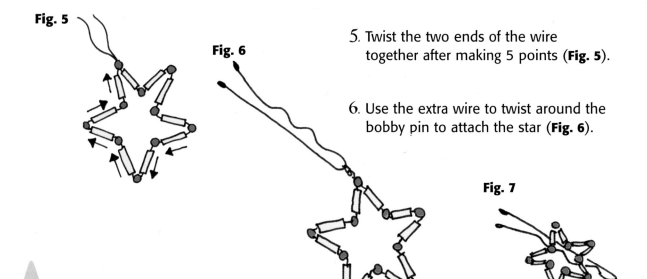

Fig. 5

Fig. 6

Fig. 7

5. Twist the two ends of the wire together after making 5 points (**Fig. 5**).

6. Use the extra wire to twist around the bobby pin to attach the star (**Fig. 6**).

TRY THIS

Attach the star to the middle of the bobby pin so the star doesn't hang, but sits on the pin (**Fig. 7**). Or attach the star to a necklace as a pendant or to a bracelet as a charm.

WIRE FLOWER BOBBY PIN

Fig. 1

Fig. 2

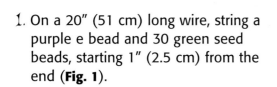

1. On a 20" (51 cm) long wire, string a purple e bead and 30 green seed beads, starting 1" (2.5 cm) from the end (**Fig. 1**).

2. Loop the wire back through the purple e bead as shown (**Fig. 2**), and pull tight, making sure that there is no extra space between beads.

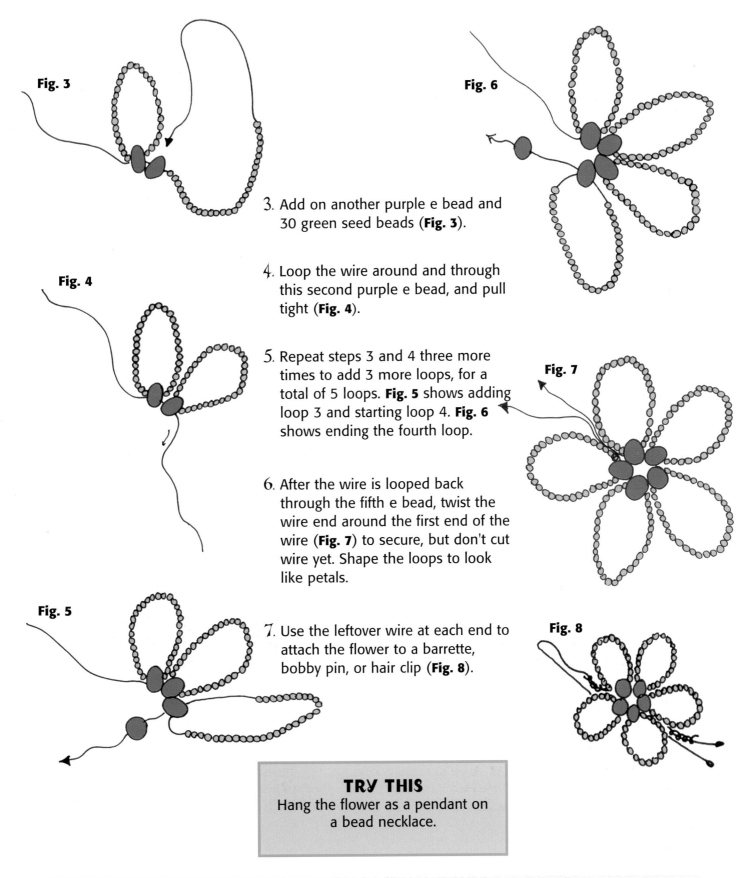

Fig. 3

Fig. 4

Fig. 5

Fig. 6

Fig. 7

Fig. 8

3. Add on another purple e bead and 30 green seed beads (**Fig. 3**).

4. Loop the wire around and through this second purple e bead, and pull tight (**Fig. 4**).

5. Repeat steps 3 and 4 three more times to add 3 more loops, for a total of 5 loops. **Fig. 5** shows adding loop 3 and starting loop 4. **Fig. 6** shows ending the fourth loop.

6. After the wire is looped back through the fifth e bead, twist the wire end around the first end of the wire (**Fig. 7**) to secure, but don't cut wire yet. Shape the loops to look like petals.

7. Use the leftover wire at each end to attach the flower to a barrette, bobby pin, or hair clip (**Fig. 8**).

TRY THIS
Hang the flower as a pendant on a bead necklace.

WIRE BUTTERFLY BOBBY PIN

YOU WILL NEED

Light purple seed beads
Royal blue seed beads
Iridescent blue-black seed beads
Silver e beads
Wire (24 gauge)
Bobby pin, barrette, or hair clip

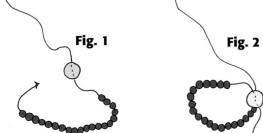

Fig. 1

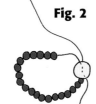

Fig. 2

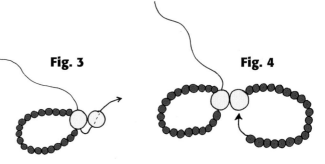

Fig. 3

Fig. 4

1. String a silver e bead and 20 blue-black seed beads onto the middle of a 20" long (51 cm) wire (**Fig. 1**).

2. Loop a wire end back through the e bead as shown (**Fig. 2**), and pull tight.

3. String another silver e bead on the same wire end (**Fig. 3**).

4. Add 20 blue-black seed beads to the same wire end and loop back through the near e bead (**Fig. 4**). Pull tight so that there is no extra space between the beads.

Fig. 5

Fig. 6

Fig. 7

Fig. 8

Fig. 9

Fig. 10

5. Add another silver e bead; then string 23 royal blue seed beads and loop the wire back through the e bead as shown (**Fig. 5**). Pull tight.

6. Using the other end of the wire, string a silver e bead (**Fig. 6**).

7. String 23 royal blue seed beads, loop the wire back through the silver e bead as shown (**Fig. 7**), and pull tight.

8. Take both ends of the wires and make two twists close to the top two silver e beads (**Fig. 8**).

9. Add 14 light purple seed beads to each wire end (**Fig. 9**).

10. One bead before the last bead, twist each wire end around the wire, to secure the seed beads (**Fig. 10**). Cut off excess wire.

11. Shape the wires to look like butterfly wings and antennae.

12. Use another piece of wire to attach the butterfly to a barrette or bobby pin.

TRY THIS
Make another butterfly in another color combination.

DRAGONFLY BOBBY PIN

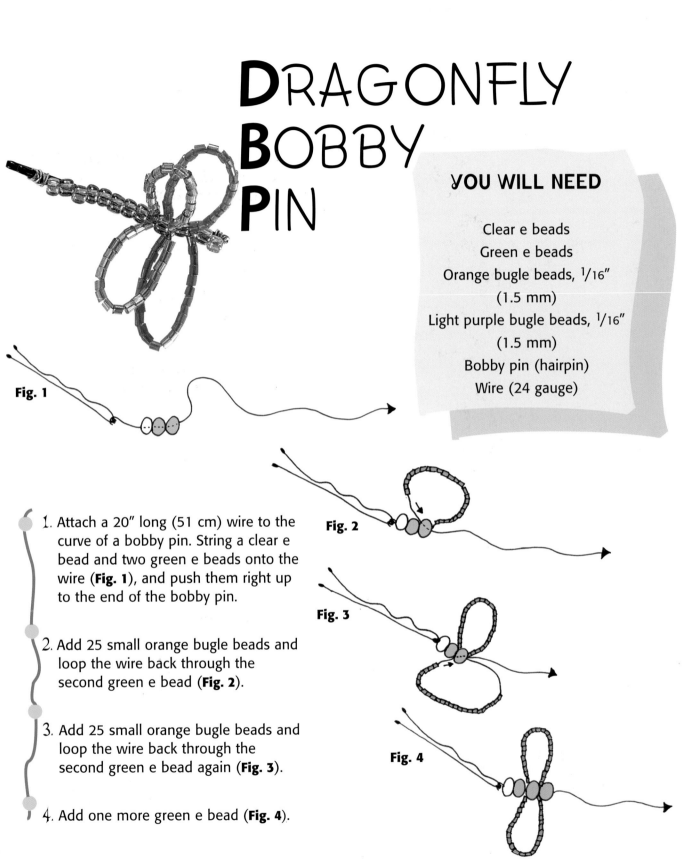

YOU WILL NEED

Clear e beads
Green e beads
Orange bugle beads, 1/16″
(1.5 mm)
Light purple bugle beads, 1/16″
(1.5 mm)
Bobby pin (hairpin)
Wire (24 gauge)

Fig. 1

Fig. 2

Fig. 3

Fig. 4

1. Attach a 20″ long (51 cm) wire to the curve of a bobby pin. String a clear e bead and two green e beads onto the wire (**Fig. 1**), and push them right up to the end of the bobby pin.

2. Add 25 small orange bugle beads and loop the wire back through the second green e bead (**Fig. 2**).

3. Add 25 small orange bugle beads and loop the wire back through the second green e bead again (**Fig. 3**).

4. Add one more green e bead (**Fig. 4**).

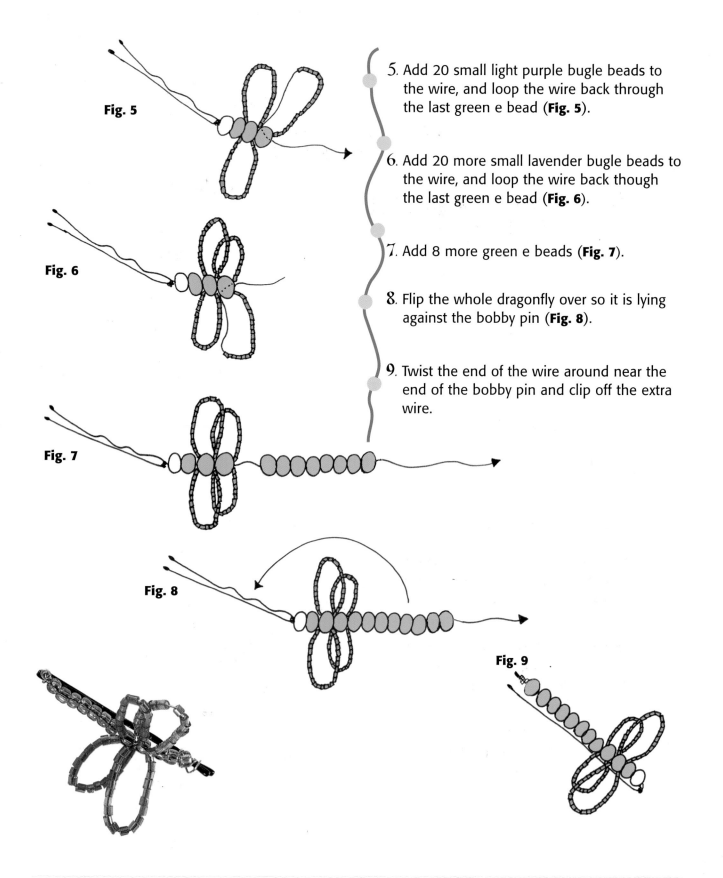

Fig. 5

5. Add 20 small light purple bugle beads to the wire, and loop the wire back through the last green e bead (**Fig. 5**).

Fig. 6

6. Add 20 more small lavender bugle beads to the wire, and loop the wire back though the last green e bead (**Fig. 6**).

Fig. 7

7. Add 8 more green e beads (**Fig. 7**).

Fig. 8

8. Flip the whole dragonfly over so it is lying against the bobby pin (**Fig. 8**).

9. Twist the end of the wire around near the end of the bobby pin and clip off the extra wire.

Fig. 9

INDEX

bead sizes, 7
beaded bobby pin, 68
bracelets and anklets, 39-57
braided headband, 60
bugle bead stripes barrette, 63
bugle beads, 7, 8
chain of flowers bracelet, 44
circles necklace, 20
clasps, 9
coiled snake bracelet, 43
crossing strands bracelet, 42
curling tail necklace, 18
dangling bead bobby pin, 60
dangling bug bobby pin, 69
diamonds bracelet, 48
dragonfly bobby pin, 78
e beads, 7
elastic thread, 9
festive stripes barrette, 66
floating beads necklace, 16
flowers and leaves necklace, 34
flowers out of line necklace, 36
glue, 8
hair ornaments, 59-79
hanging bugle beads necklace, 22
hanging circles anklet, 56
hanging loops necklace, 26
hanging wire star bobby pin, 72
icicles necklace, 30

knots, 10
linking loops necklace, 28
multi-strand choker, 32
neatening ends of thread
   or wire, 11
necklaces, 13-37
needles, 9
overhand knot, 10
pliers, 9
pony beads, 8
Roman headband, 62
running out of thread, 11
seed beads, 7
simply beads necklace, 14
squares bracelet, 46
squiggles bobby pin, 71
sunshine necklace, 24
techno triangles bracelet, 52
threads, 8, 10
triangles bracelet, 50
twice as nice necklace, 15
twister barrette, 63
two-tailed necklace, 17
waves and pearls anklet, 54
wire butterfly bobby pin, 76
wire ends, 10
wire flower bobby pin, 74
wire, 8, 10
zigzag flowers bracelet, 40